Borders
Tales and Trails

Kenneth Turnbull
with
Norman Turnbull

Durham, NC

Borders Tales and Trails
Kenneth Turnbull with Norman Turnbull

Published 2018, by Torchflame Books
an Imprint of Light Messages
www. lightmessages. com
Durham, NC 27713 USA
SAN: 920-9298

Paperback ISBN: 978-1-61153-206-7
Ebook ISBN: 978-1-61153-205-0
Library of Congress Control Number: 2018908322

Except as noted, the photographs used in this book are by the authors and a number of outstanding photographers who have graciously made them available for use by licence from Creative Commons, a non-profit organization devoted to providing creative works for others to use, build upon, and share. The cover image of Smailholm Tower is by Georgethefourth licenced from Shutterstock.

Dedicated to

the memory of Norman Turnbull,
those who call the Borders home,
and those in whose hearts its memory persists from afar.

Contents

Foreword

The story of Scotland is that of a brave and defiant people's desire for self-determination. The recorded part of that story covers thousands of years and involves much internal strife and frequent wars with great foreign powers, including the Vikings, Romans, and English. That a nation so small could survive under such conditions, evolve, and thrive to become influential to the entire world, is a testament to the power of human will and courage.

The events and characters of that story are far too many for this book, indeed any single book. Our goal is not to cover or even summarise the history of Scotland or the Scottish Borders. We seek only to provide a glimpse of some of the people, places and events of note to the Borders, with a few remarks on how they came to be, and what exists today.

We view events primarily through the history of one Borders family; the Turnbulls. That family, or clan as Borders families have come to be known, serves as an example of all Borders clans.

It is a character of the Scots that most consider themselves and their clans to be unique and special. In truth, like others, the Turnbulls share more in common than differences with their neighbours; the Armstrongs, Bells, Cecils, Croziers, Dodds, Douglases, Elliotts, Fenwicks, Forsters, Grahams, Homes, Howards, Irvines, Johnstones, Kerrs, Maxwells, Murrays, Nixons, Riddels, Robsons, Rutherfords, Scotts, Storeys, Stuarts, Taits, and others.

For the adventurous ones who choose to take any of the trails described in this book, it is hoped that Norman's personal research to these historic sites, will be interesting and give the reader an insight into the earlier times of the Borders region. Visitors should gain more of an understanding of the rugged terrain and the scenic points where these events occurred, from a Scotsman who has been there.

We have included more castles and battle sites than most visitors will be able to or wish to visit. Remember, however, that most fortifications including castles and Borders towers were strategically placed on high ground with a view of the surrounding countryside. Even if you have seen enough castles or if the history of some does not interest you, the view each provides is unique and an ideal way to see and sense the glorious territory that is the Borders of Scotland.

There are many peel towers known as Borders tower houses in the Scottish Marches. Residents in respect for and celebration of their heritage have lovingly restored a number of them as homes. We include only a few towers that are proudly called Castles by the Borderers and serve as examples, sometimes chosen from the perspective of the illustrative clan.

A number of Borders residences and hotels are also commonly called 'castles.' Many of those are magnificent buildings and grounds worth visiting, but we only include those with a military history, except for Floors Castle in Kelso, which is considered a touristic highlight.

We do not make any claim to completeness in this work. Many omissions have been made consciously for the sake of practicality. Not all events, people, or places of importance to the Borders have been covered. Alternate, perhaps preferred, examples might exist. Those used were chosen from the perspective of the illustrative clan.

Preface

By Kenneth Turnbull

Norman Turnbull was born in Edinburgh in 1942 and grew up in the countryside, on a farm near the Borders. At the age of 18, he put aside his love of the countryside for the loyalty of his country and enlisted in the Royal Air Force. On return from his service, he worked at several jobs around Leeds in England.

Norman eventually returned to Scotland where, in his own words, 'I have, throughout my life, had a strong feeling that my surname had a part in the history of the Borders.'

In 2009, Norman worked closely with the local Borders Turnbull Clan Association in the preparations for the international clan gathering and the unveiling of the famous *Turning of the Bull* monument at the Hawick Heritage Hub. He was instrumental in producing a historical video, which included a history of Scotland and the Turnbull Clan. Norman was appointed as Clan High Shanachie by the Turnbull Clan Association in 2010.

Sadly, the Turnbull Clan lost a valuable member, when, at the age of 71, Norman lost his battle with cancer in June 2013. He was a true gentleman who wanted nothing more than to serve his fellow clansmen and help preserve their history.

In keeping with Norman's wishes, as Clan Vice Chairman and Editor of Turnbull Clan Association publications, I have organised and expanded Norman's manuscript and notes into this volume.

Neither Norman nor I have attempted to cover the entire history of

Scotland. We sought only to provide a glimpse of the history, people, and events of the region of Scotland known as the Borders. This has been done through the perspective of one clan, the Turnbulls, as representative of those who have called this difficult but compelling land home.

Your ancestors may have been Turnbulls, their neighbours; the Armstrongs, Elliotts, Grahams, Kerrs, Rutherfords, Scotts, or others. They may have been from other parts of Scotland. Perhaps you merely want to know a wee bit about how this place and its people came to be. Whatever the case, I hope you will enjoy this book and be motivated to learn more about the resilient nation of Scotland and its tenacious people.

By Norman Turnbull

In the early days of Scotland, only the head of the family had an identity. The rest of the family were known as the wife of ..., the son of ..., or the daughter of .... A surname was a family designation to be added later to identify the clan or *clann* in Gaelic, meaning children.

All this was something I had never given thought to, until I attended a clan gathering of the Turnbulls in a small village called Denholm in the Scottish Borders, just outside Hawick. It was here that I met up with other people with the Turnbull name. That started my curiosity. I made up my mind, there and then, that I wanted to find out more about my heritage and from where I came. So, I joined the Turnbull Clan Association and began studying my history and that of my Borders people.

In my lifetime, I have travelled to and lived in many places, but never felt settled until I returned to the Borders where for once, I felt at peace with myself. Not understanding why this should be, I took up employment, as a hill shepherd on Harwood Estate, near Bonchester Bridge.

I learned that the land that I was living on and working upon was the same land that had once belonged to my clan. I understood why I was experiencing such a feeling of peacefulness. I was back living and working in the valley of the Rulewater, in the shadow of Rubers Law, the home of my ancestors. The feel, smell, and taste of the land awoke an unknown memory from deep in my soul and DNA.

Kenneth Turnbull

Alastair Cunningham - Scottish Clans and Castles Ltd.

Clans and Castles of Scotland

Way Back

Earthquakes and volcanic eruptions shaped Scotland forty million years ago. After four ice ages, the land became split and eroded. As the last ice age melted, straths and glens formed.

Colin - Wikimedia Commons - CC BY-SA 4.0

The Land

Palaeomagnetic studies of the Earth's magnetic field in rocks and the composition of those rocks indicate that several hundred million years ago, the island of Great Britain was divided between two separate continents. Part of Scotland was on Laurentia, which has become North America and the rest was part of Gondwana near the South Pole.

Eighteen thousand years ago, during the last ice age, the land was buried under a vast sheet of ice 756 feet thick and obliterated any trace of life that might have pre-existed.

Three thousand years passed, then, gradually the temperature began to rise. The ice sheets groaned and cracked and retreated northwards. In the short space of only a few hundred years, they had disappeared entirely.

The largest part of Scotland, at the end of the Ice Age, became covered in dense forest. The northern part of Scotland became the Caledonian Forest. Today, only one per cent of the original forest covers around 111 square miles in isolated locations across Scotland. On the West Coast, oak and birch predominated in a temperate rainforest, rich in fern, moss, and lichens.

The Caledonian Forest was home to a wide variety of wildlife, much of which was not found elsewhere in the British Isles including wild boar, brown bear, Eurasian lynx, grey wolf, elk, aurochs, (wild cattle) and tarpans (wild horses).

Over time, the constant wet and windy influences were ideal for the development of a wide range of wetlands, especially around the borders. The land formations around the borders were lower and undulating, compared to the many mountainous areas of the highlands. These wetlands were famed for their bogs, peat and moss-covered hills.

The landmass of Scotland today consists of some twenty million acres, but less than a quarter is good enough to support habitation. A million acres are taken up with fresh water and foreshore, another million covered in forest. On eleven million acres nothing can grow. The spine of Scotland forms a natural barrier with the watershed between the Atlantic Ocean and the North Sea.

Indigenous People

Human settlements in Scotland began roughly 12,000 years ago during the Stone Age. Early colonisation took place by vastly different cultures through a land bridge now beneath the English Channel, from the north, through the islands now known as the Shetlands and the Orkneys, and from Ireland to the west.

One of the earliest known permanent settlements in Scotland is a small area about 20 miles south-west of Aberdeen called Balbridie, which was settled between 3400 and 4000 BC.

Kenneth Turnbull

A Pictish stone from Invereen.
The carved symbols are typical of the 7th c. and 8th c.
The meanings are unknown.
Edinburgh Museum

The Celtic tribe of Picts with strong DNA similarities to the Basque peoples of Northern Europe began as a stone-age society and built settlements at Maes Howe and Skara Brae on Orkney, which date back to 3200 BC. Later, the Irish Celtic tribe of Gaels settled western Scotland.

Communities from the beginning hugged the fertile coastal areas, and for centuries, the easiest way to make contact was by sea. This resulted in the land becoming a patchwork of dialects and customs.

Most of the terrain was not ideal for the growing of crops. The land was best suited to grazing cattle and sheep, and even then, grazing was patchy in the lower regions. Scotland was a rural society. Products included skins, grain, wool and coal and these in the main, were used for trading and export.

The Roman Empire

Scotland's history was better recorded after the arrival of the Romans. With their empire stretching through Europe and the province of Britannia (England) the Romans repeatedly attempted to colonise Scotland, which they called *Caledonia*. It is said that the word derived from the early Celtic language *Caleto* (hard or strong) and was a name used by a tribal confederation of native Picts.

From the mid-first century through the second century, the Romans repeatedly invaded Caledonia. They won battles and established fortifications, but they could not colonise the Caledonian people. According to the Roman historian Tacitus, Calgacus, leader of the native tribes resisting the Roman advance in Scotland (79-83 AD) declared, 'Caledonians … the last men on Earth, the last of the free.'

The Romans built two barrier walls; one known as Hadrian's Wall, begun in 122 AD, it formed the northernmost frontier of the Roman Empire. This wall was fortified from the west coast to the east coast, some 80 Roman miles long separating the two cultures. A second, the Antonine Wall, 38 miles long, was begun in 142 AD but was abandoned nine years later, with the death of Antoninus Pius. The Caledonian lands north of Hadrian's Wall were known as *Pictavia* (Pictland) at that time.

At the Romans third and last major invasion attempt, they encountered the reformed insurgent tribes, known as the Picts. These wild painted people, small in stature, who wore almost no clothing, were more savage than the Romans had ever fought. So, after 300 years of trying to colonise these tribes, the Romans finally retreated behind their walls and Caledonia remained unconquered. Remaining sections of both walls can still be seen today.

Mixed Cultures

Between the invasions of the 5th and 8th centuries, several population groups developed in Caledonia. The Lowland Scot is primarily of Anglo-Saxon stock. To the north and west, is the Scotland of the Gaelic Highlander. In the Orkney and Shetland Islands, the culture is akin to Scandinavia through Norse invasion, followed by colonisation. The Orkney Islands provided the ideal base for plundering throughout Scotland and along the coastlines of Britain.

The extent to which these settlers replaced or mixed with the native populations and to contribute to the genetic make-up of Scotland remains undecided. The past is alive and remains part of everyday life, albeit unconsciously. Celtic, Norse and Viking colonisation have made a lasting impression in Scotland. Evidence of this is found in place names, language, genetics and other facets of cultural heritage, as well as in the DNA of the people.

Geography conspired to make the creation of a nation difficult. Hence the struggle to overcome the barriers of nature made the Scottish unity and nationhood, once achieved, more precious.

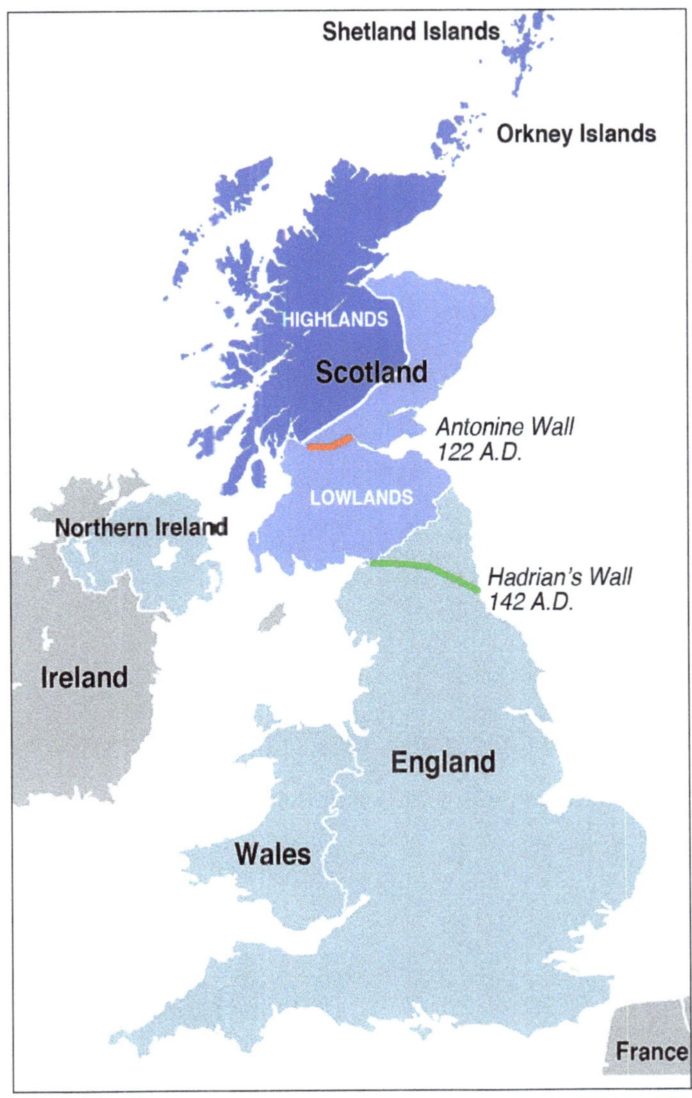

Kenneth Turnbull

Scotland's landmass on Britain showing the two walls built by the Romans

The evolution of castles throughout Scotland began, both as fortifications and as secure dwellings for lords and nobles during the 12th century. This was the beginning of feudal land tenure during the reign of Alexander I (1107-24). David I, was even more influential in the development of castles, especially in the Scottish Lowlands.

The earliest Scottish castles were initially constructed of dirt and wood on raised mounds of earth and known as a *motte* by the French. They included a wooden tower or fortress enclosing a courtyard, usually over a *fosse* (ditch) which surrounded all sides. These early castles had a single entrance via a wooden bridge.

Kenneth. Turnbull

A section of Hadrian's wall at Homesteads, England

Kenneth. Turnbull

The eastern end mound remains of Antonine wall at Falkirk, Scotland

Borders

Painting by W. Turnbull -

The Scottish Borders are situated along the eastern part of the Southern Uplands. The region is hilly and mostly rural, with the River Tweed flowing west to east through it.

Central Borders

The term 'Central Borders' refers to the area in which the majority of the main towns including Galashiels, Selkirk, Hawick, Jedburgh, Earlston, Kelso, Newtown St. Boswells, Peebles, Melrose and Tweedbank are located. Many of those towns lie along the River Tweed that flows through the area, forming a natural border.

Historically, the term 'Borders' has a wider meaning, referring to all of the burghs near the English border, which includes those of Dumfriesshire and Kirkcudbrightshire as well as Northumberland, Cumberland and Westmorland in England.

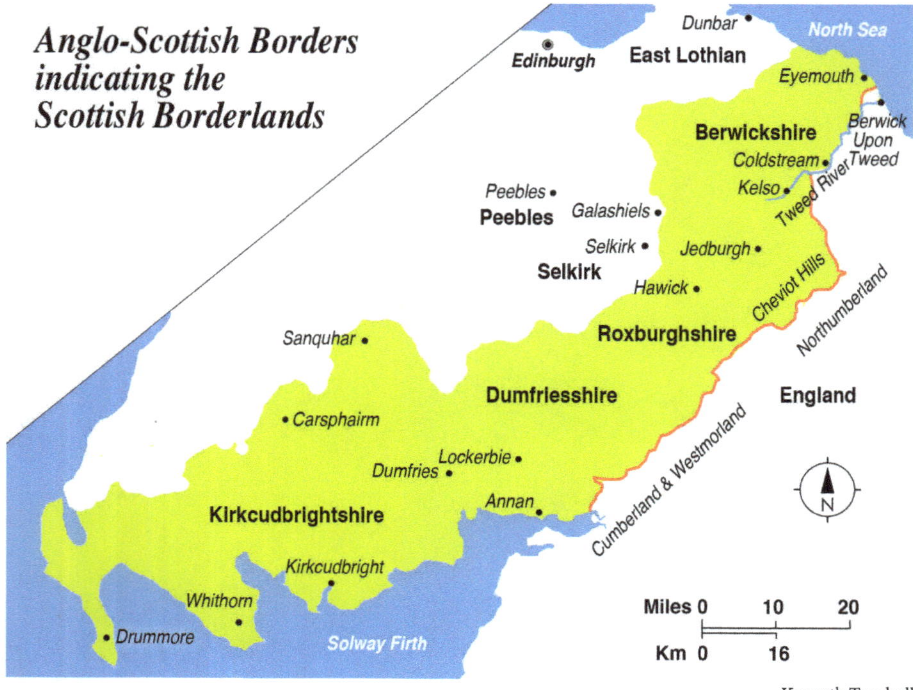

Kenneth Turnbull

Roxburghshire and Berwickshire bore the brunt of the conflicts with England, both during declared wars such as the Wars of Scottish Independence and armed raids, which took place in the times of the Border reivers. As a result, the ruins of many castles, abbeys, even towns can still be seen in those regions.

The history of the Borders on both sides is a difficult one to follow, as many of the battles for power between England and Scotland were fought to the north or south of a changing boundary. Even in the earlier Roman times, the Borders of Scotland remained undecided. It wasn't until 1018 that the traditional Scottish border, from the River Tweed across to the Firth of Forth, was finally granted to the Scottish Kingdom. But there were many border disputes yet to be encountered.

Rule and Rulewater

Regulas Roule or Rule was a monk or Saint from a town called Patras, 133 miles west of Athens. Scottish legend has it that during the 12th century, he became shipwrecked on the shores of Fife, at a place called Kilrymont, which is now St. Andrews. He had with him several bones of Saint Andrew. Angus, the Pictish king, who lived in either the 8th or 9th century, welcomed him. By the 11th century, the name of Rule had become well-known and widespread. Some believe that the Borders Clan Rule derived their name from Saint Rule, but that is unlikely.

Like other Borders families, the origins of the Turnbull Clan are uncertain and probably mixed. Use of the name 'DeRule' as well as 'Rule' in early documents, indicates that perhaps the original name of the clan was that of DeRule, a Norman knight who accompanied William the Conqueror in his 11th-century invasion of England. DeRule would have been French-Norman for 'of Rolo,' the Viking who became the first Duke of Normandy.

Hector Boece, the Scottish historian, notes in the Wars of Scottish Independence, that in the 10th and 11th centuries, Vikings settled the lands from where the Rule-Turnbulls came. Thus, giving them a very Norse look and who were described to be of 'great size, many having blonde and red hair and prominent blue eyes.

Another possibility is that the Rule family took their name from the Rulewater River along which they lived. The Borderland home of the Rule-Tunbull clan is located in the eastern part of the southern uplands, which is one of the least populous areas of Scotland. The landform is undulating with patches of low-lying land and a scattering of hills. From the source of the Rulewater River to the confluence of the Teviot River, the Rule-Turnbull clan occupied almost all of the lands in that area.

Robert Burns, John Leyden, and Sir Walter Scott wrote romantic stories, poems, and ballads about the Borders and its heroes such as Kinmont Willie Armstrong, and William Rule Turnbull, but in reality, it was far from romantic. The life of a border clansman was more difficult than what we might imagine in this modern day. Danger came from all sides, not only from the English Crown, but also between the clans. It was a life of constant fear, extreme hardships, and hunger.

Rubers Law and the Rulewater Valley

W. Turnbull - CC SA 3.0

The Rulewater Valley runs just eight miles north of England. The name Rule of the Rulewater is composed of two Gaelic words. *Ruchd-Thuil* pronounced *Ruch-oul* and contracted into 'Roull' which means the rumbling-noised river, which fittingly describes the sound of the stream as it flows through the valley into the Teviot River that, in turn, flows into the Tweed.

Bhaile, in Gaelic, signifies a small settlement well placed in an otherwise rough terrain. This appropriately describes a number of hamlets in the valley along the Rulewater; Hall of Roull, Toun of Roull (Town-o'-Rule) Abbott Roull (Abbotrule) and Bad Roull (Bedrule).

The Town-o'-Rule on the Hallrule estate, is a name of ancient times and appears in the old ecclesiastical records of Jedburgh Abbey. The Town-o'-Rule shaped a large part of the extensive Barony of Feu-rule and occupied the whole breadth of Hobkirk parish. Regarded as the main town in the district and a very important one, too.

The first authentic record of the name appears in 1128, concerning persons named Adam Roule, Richard Roule, William Roule and John Roule. These are noted in the Scottish border county of Roxburgh. The name again appears in the same county about 1214.

Many members of the Rule family were landholders in the 12th, 13th, and 14th centuries. Several families also held titles and bore coats of arms. Between 1214 and 1249, the first clan chiefs were Alan Roule and Richard, his son.

Most individuals were known only by their given name and the area where they came, as in this case 'of Rule' as a surname. In 1313, Will-o'-Rule, a resident of Rule, was the one who was responsible for giving the Turnbull Clan its name when King Robert the Bruce changed his name to Turn-e-bull. Following this, the use of Rule as a surname dwindled, while the use of Turn-e-bull increased.

Remains of the original Abbotrule Kirk left and parsonage below

Betty Turnbull - CC SA 3.0

Turnbull Clan holdings expanded to include Mynto (Minto) estate four miles to the north of Bedrule near Denholm. King David II corroborated these lands before 1370. Tensions began when a John Turnbull became Lord of Minto through marriage and the granting of this title by Stewart of Jedworth in 1390. He had an obstinate temperament and was nicknamed as, 'Out with Swerd.'

John Turnbull, together with Sir William Stewart, were often involved in plundering raids over the border. In 1399, they were taken prisoner and committed to the Tower of London for fourteen years and, as a consequence, lost title to their lands. John Turnbull returned to Scotland and was killed in 1424. The appointed Sheriff of Teviotdale eventually returned one-third of the lands to the Stewarts and two-thirds to the Turnbulls.

The town of Philiphaugh, north of Hawick and around 2 miles west of Selkirk, played an important role in Scotland's Borders history. The Ettrick Forest rich lands of Philiphaugh were awarded to the first Turnbull (Will-o-Rule) in 1315 and recorded as remaining in the family name in part, for 257 years.

Border Reivers

In the barbarous and dangerous days from the late 13th century to the beginning of the 17th century, the dividing border with England was unsettled and became a battleground between contending forces. Lawlessness existed around the boundaries. Raiding parties, known as 'reivers,' existed on both sides and were constantly plundering each other and causing havoc. Reive is a derivation of the Northumbrian Scots verb *reifen*, (to rob). The modern English words 'ruffian' and 'bereaved' come to us from the reivers.

Raiding and pillaging evolved from political rivalry into a business of sorts, providing a way of life in difficult times. Allegiances shifted, and clans switched their support from one nation to the other, as suited their interests at that time. Because national allegiances were often absent, the violence was not only international, but it included feuds, bitterness and fighting between the clans.

wikipedia.org curid 3749294

Painting of Border Reivers by Tom Scott
Mainhill Gallery, Ancrum

Reiving wasn't regarded as thievery by the reivers because they took from the enemy. This was a way to survive in those harsh times. If a reiver's family needed something they would simply make a raid on an estate, farm, or home and take what they needed, be it sheep, grain, cattle, or even women.

Reiving to steal cattle was commonplace. To curtail this, border riding became a regular and essential way of protecting the community-based common lands from trespassing by rivals. An appointed person would regularly ride around the boundaries to claim the area and prevent infringement.

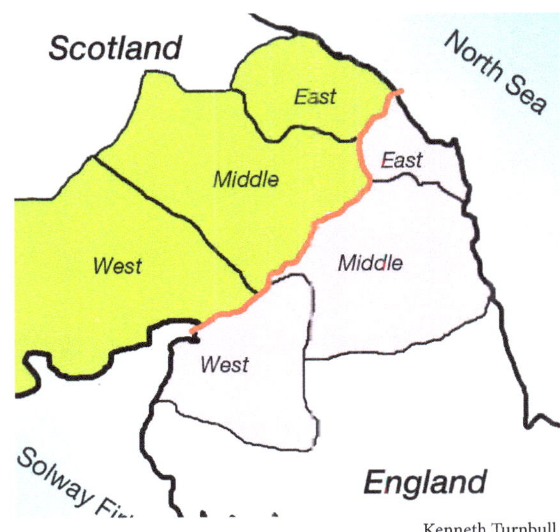

The six divisions of the Scottish Marches Treaty

Border riding continued after it was no longer necessary and became known as Common Riding, which has now developed into an annual tradition to commemorate this history. Hawick is one of many border towns to have kept up this tradition.

The battleground along the Borders needed to be contained, so the Marches were conceived in a treaty between Henry III of England and Alexander III of Scotland in 1249. The aim was to control the Anglo-Scottish border by providing a buffer zone called the West, Middle, and East Marches, equally dividing both sides of the Anglo-Scottish border.

In the late 13th century, Edward of England appointed the first Lord Warden of the Marches, whose task was to oversee these regions and keep the domain secure.

About 20 miles to the southeast of Hawick, the top of Carter Bar is situated on the border between the nations. It was here that frequent meetings took place between the Scottish and English Wardens of the Marches to deal with grievances and criminal offences between various clans on either side of the border.

Along these border there existed some Debatable Lands, claimed by both Scotland and England as part of their national territory. There were two renowned areas of contention. The largest was at the eastern boundary at the Solway Firth and the second, along the northeastern boundary at the North Sea. For a time, powerful local clans dominated the region on the border between England and Scotland, where neither monarch's writ was heeded.

Disputes over this land occurred over many generations and as a result, it became a refuge for all types of people, because there was no obedience to either crown. It was seen as 'no man's land' and was used as a place of escape from justice. The population of these areas included murderers, rapists, vagabonds, thieves, and men who had been stripped of their names.

Of course, being a lawless land meant that the people had to be ever vigilant in protecting themselves and their property from one another. Despite this, there were many settlements from the Solway Firth boundary near Carlisle to Langholm in Dumfries and Galloway, Canonbie being the largest populated area in the region.

For over 300 years, the border clansmen controlled these areas. The Armstrongs were the strongest clan in the Debatable Lands. They were known to be capable of putting 3,000 men in the field of battle at any given time, They were the most feared horse-riding clan on the Borders. The law, if any, would have been Armstrong's Law. An innocent traveller would likely have given those debatable lands a wide berth and travelled from the north to the south via the eastern edge of the countries.

The Douglasses were the most prominent and powerful of the border clans, possessing the most lands. During the latter part of the Middle Ages, they often held the power behind the throne of the Stewart kings.

The Kerrs were a significant force within the Borderlands and a prominent reiver clan. Their territories were large and many. There were two branches of the well-known clan who often feuded with the Scott's clan, as well as with each other. In the 16th century, both Andrew Kerr of Ferniehurst and Andrew Kerr of Cessford were made Wardens of the Middle Marches.

The Kerrs were predominantly left-handed, which gave them an advantage in sword fighting. They owned several castles including Ferniehirst Castle, built in 1470, just south of Jedburgh, complete with a famous left-handed staircase. To this day, being Kerr-handed means to be left-handed.

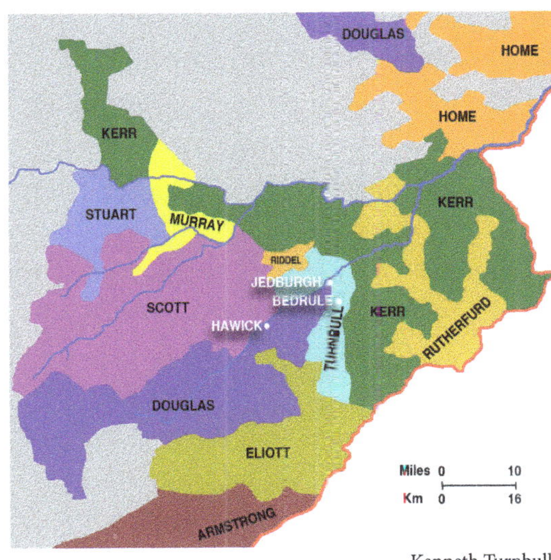

Kenneth Turnbull

The clans early claims to land ownership along the borders

The Scotts were a very powerful clan family, serving both as Border reivers as well as ruling officers. Many Scotts families lived at Scotstown and Kirkurd, within the county of Peebles.

The Elliot clan though fewer in number, were important and notable Border reivers.

Rutherford is one of the most ancient surnames of Scotland. The clan was known for their extensive land ownership and border raids into Northumberland. John Rutherford's son Daniel, and the uncle of the novelist Sir Walter Scott, was the discoverer of nitrogen in 1772.

The Turnbulls were one of the most formidable and lawless of the Borders reiver clans, often at feud with their Kerr neighbours. It was said, 'there is no fight without a Turnbull and no Turnbull without a fight.' When one Scottish aristocrat, sent to see if they would back his claim to the throne, the Turnbulls replied that they had, 'no care at all for politicians, but always longed for a fight.'

Bishop William Turnbull founded the University of Glasgow in 1451. Today, it is one of the oldest Universities in the English speaking world with around 18,000 undergraduates and some 7,000 postgraduates from over 120 countries.

Other clan names linked with the Borders include; Anderson, Bruce, Burn, Davison, Gilchrist, Laidlaw, Murray, Oliver, Pringle, Tait, Thomson, Turner, Henderson and Young. Many other clans were also based in the Borders, but being unable to cover everything, we concentrate our attention on Roxburghshire and Berwickshire.

It wasn't until 1530 that King James V acted against the lawlessness of the Debatable Lands. He imprisoned Lords Bothwell, Maxwell and

Home, Walter Scott of Buccleuch and various other border Lairds for their lack of action against the men of the Debatable Lands.

However, the most significant action he made, was the capture and hanging of Johnnie Armstrong of Gilnockie, along with 31 other men at Carlanrig Chapel. Word had it that the circumstances were questionable. As a result, Crown Officers of England and Wales in the following year came up with a proclamation in another attempt to quell the Debatable lands as follows. In part, it proclaimed …

> All Englishmen and Scotsmen, after this proclamation made, are and shall be free to rob, burn, spoil, slay, murder and destroy all and every such persons, their bodies, buildings, goods and cattle as do remain or shall inhabit upon any part of the said debatable land without any redress to be made for the same.[1]

That was an open message for free-for-all plundering. However, even this did not work. So, it was agreed in 1552 (by commissioners) that a dike, known as the Scots Dyke, should be built to mark the boundary. Again, this did not stop the lawlessness. Only when King James VI of Scotland became King James the 1st of England and united the two countries did the face of the border clans change with the Pacification of the Borders policy, which destroyed fortified tower houses and rounded up families to be sent to Ireland and elsewhere.

The Borderers had a way of life that, in many ways, resembled that of the Highlanders. Their society was clan-like in structure. Council decrees and legal disputes were often related to specific surnames such as Armstrong, Scott, Elliot and Turnbull.

Borderers were mostly of Protestant faith. They were either Presbyterian or Nonconformist evangelical and their language was Scots, rather than Gaelic. They kept many connections with the Northumbrian and Cumbrian English speakers on the south side of the border, though their ancient role as frontier guards had excused and supported a lifestyle of raiding on each other.

Apart from fighting for Scotland's independence, the border clans

---

1 Gerard Carruthers and David Goldie Editors, *Scotland and the 19th-Century World,* (New York: Rodopi, 2012), 82.

often fought among themselves for survival. The terrain of the Borderlands was not suitable for the growth of most crops. Grazing cattle and sheep, was what the land was most suited for, and even the grazing was patchy in the lower regions. Raiding and pillaging was a way of surviving, which caused feuds and bitterness between clans.

To carry the name of a clan family was very important. A man would fight to the death to protect his name. A man who betrayed his clan could have his name taken away from him. Without a name, he was seen as non-existing and was fair prey.

For almost 300 years, inhabitants of the Scottish Borders lived in a territory dividing two nations at war. Periods of peace were so few and so brief that the inhabitants subsisted in an atmosphere of almost constant conflict. Even in the so-called peace times, the people were still exposed to freebooting raids from southern neighbours, yet none looked to a Scots king, or his government, for protection, compensation, or revenge.

The unsettled state of the Borders and the lawlessness of the clans did not help the establishment of a permanent peace between the nations, despite many attempts by both governments. A complete overhaul of the whole social structure of the border area took time after the union of the crowns.

King James I/VI knew it would be no easy task to convert the turbulent clans into law-abiding citizens, so vigorous and ruthless methods were adopted. Wardens of the Marches on both sides of the borderline were ordered to use hostility in an aggressive manner against the malefactors and to punish by death, or banish, all who would not conform.

The most influential men in the area had to sign an undertaking to assist the king's officers, and among them were the Turnbulls of Bedrule, Minto and Wauchope. The natives had never experienced such a strict control. Many were outlawed and either fled the district or joined mercenary bands on the continent. One such group consisted of 200 legionnaires, who enlisted under Scott of Buccleuch to assist the Netherlands in their war with Spain. Among the declared fugitives, whose whereabouts were henceforth unknown, was George Turnbull, Son of James of Westlees, and Gavin, son of the Laird of Bedrule.

Arms of the Turnbull Clan Association

During their early occupation of Philiphaugh, in the Ettrick Valley, one John Turnbull has been mentioned in 1360, as Sheriff of Selkirkshire, and four years later, another of the family name held the post as Deputy Sheriff. Those were the only early occasions in which the Turnbulls were credited in connection with the administration of the law.

In 1461, the Murrays acquired part of the Philiphaugh lands, and the properties became further merged after the marriage of Murray to a Turnbull daughter.

After two of the Philiphaugh families were slain at Flodden, with another in Spain, the estate slowly declined. When the last of the Philiphaugh Turnbulls died in 1572, what was left, fell into Murray possession.

The last of the border frays took place on 7th June 1575, at Reidswire, on the bleak moorland of the Carter Bar, where Scotland and England meet. It was the day when the wardens of the respective marches met to settle disputes, redress wrongs, and arrange compensation for proven thefts from either side.

Allegations of unfair treatment caused resentment and the men from Redesdale and Tynedale on the English side of the borderline discharged a hail of arrows among the Scots bystanders. Just then, a body of Jedburgh citizens arrived, as pent-up emotions were released into a gory conflict that became the subject of Borders ballads.

Little harness had we thair;
But auld Badrule had on a jack,
and did richt weil, I you declare,
Wi' all the Turnbulls at his back
Gude Ederstane was not to lack,
With Kirktoun, Newtoun, nobill men.

Thir is ail the specials I hais spack,
For by them that I could nocht ken.

Quha did invent that day of play,
We neid nocht feir to find him sune,
For Sir John Foster, I dar weil say,
Maid us that noysome afternune:
Not that I speik precisely out,
That he supposd it wald be perill,
But pryde and breaking out, but dout,
Gart Tyndall lads begin the quarrell.[2]

Petty crime continued by a few of the outlawed men, but organised raids and disorders were mostly suppressed. By 1612, the pacification of the Borders was almost complete.

How did the Turnbulls adjust to the new life under peaceful conditions? Not very well, it appears. Those declared rebels forfeited what holdings they had in the valley, while others, including the chief branches of Bedrule and Minto, fell into financial difficulties and had to sell their properties to pay for their debts.

In the valuation roll of 1643, some 26 Turnbulls were assessed for land in the parishes of Abbotrule, Bedrule, Cavers, Hopkirk and Kirkton, lying on or near the Rule Water. By 1811, the number had dwindled to two; one in Hopkirk parish and the other in Kirkton. After 500 years of calling the area home, no one of the Turnbull name was recorded in Bedrule.

One prominent Turnbull, Laird Adam of Denesyde, favoured the Stuarts in the rebellion in 1715. When the cause was lost, he sold Denesyde to Sir Gilbert Elliot of Stobs. In parting, he expressed a wish that Mary's well on the roadside of the property was to remain as a public source of water as a service to the population and in memory of Queen Mary who drank the cold water from that spring. Adam moved his family to the 'Debatable Lands' of Northumberland, near Tyneside. Some of his descendants immigrated to Canada, where

2 Sir George Douglas, *A History of the Border Counties* (Roxburgh, Selkirk, Peebles) Ballad of the Raid of the Reidswire (Edinburgh: William Blackwood and Sons, 1899), 26-27.

they became prosperous wheat farmers.

As a result of their open defiance to the Crown, a bounty was placed on the head of the Borders Turnbulls, so some changed their name to Trumbull, Trimble, Tremble, Trembley, and others. Some went to France to continue fighting the English, and some went to Northern Ireland where many still live today, including David Trimble the First Minister of Northern Ireland (1998-2002). Many others emigrated to Australia, Canada, New Zealand, South Africa, the United States, and other nations.

Whether they left to flee from the law or to escape poverty, the people of Scotland made a name for themselves throughout the world out of all proportion to the population or economic importance of their homeland.

Scotland in the Twenty-First Century

The 1707 Treaty of Union with England was not popular with everyone in Scotland. From time to time the idea of reverting to independence or at least devolution gained or lost favor depending on economic and political circumstances.

Three hundred years after the Act of Union of 1707, when Scotland had voluntarily given up its right to exist independently, the nation found itself once again seeking the freedom of independent government. In 1997 a referendum for devolution received an overwhelming victory resulting in the Scottish Parliament being re-established in 1999. With this, the auld lang story of the history of Scotland, which for some, had ended in 1746 at the battle of Culloden and for others, had ended when the Bay City Rollers split up in 1978. The country had taken a new turn.

In 2014 a referendum for complete independence failed but resulted in the Scotland Act of 2016 making the parliament and government of Scotland permanent and increasing their authority.

The history of Scotland is dramatic, exciting, fascinating, bloody, at times tragic and weather wise, constantly wet and windy.

INSIDE: FULL COVERAGE OF THE OPENING OF SCOTLAND'S PARLIAMENT

THE SCOTSMAN

FRIDAY 2 JULY 1999

SCOTLAND'S NATIONAL NEWSPAPER

A moment anchored in Scotland's history

Always read the small print!

Scottish Parliament re-established

July 2, 1999

It is the Celts, Picts, Britons, Irish, Scandinavians, English, Angles, Saxons, Normans, Italians, Asians, Chinese and Poles, who have come to this land in the northern part of a small island on the edge of a small continent and made it into a nation that the Romans wanted nothing to do with.

It is a story of famous historical figures, such as Macbeth, William Wallace, Mary, Queen of Scots, and Tony Blair. It is a story of famous historical events, such as Bannockburn, Reformation, Culloden and Scotland winning the World Soccer Cup against Argentina in 1978.

The history of Scotland is also the story of the people of Scotland, the scientists, inventors, engineers, doctors and pioneers in medicine, electronics, law enforcement, transport, communications, sports, education, and economics. Through their ingenuity, the Scots have provided the world with more inventions and discoveries per-capita than any other nation including the bicycle, steam engine, macadam roads, the telephone, television, penicillin, computing origins,[3] the tractor beam, the seismometer, Dolly the cloned sheep, and the bionic heart, to name just a few.

There were also the poets, the novelists, the singers, the actors and the entertainers who contributed to the world, 'Auld Lang Syne, *Peter Pan*, *Treasure Island*, *Trainspotting*, Sherlock Holmes, soulful music, and even comic songs such as 'Donald Where's Your Troosers?'

wikimedia.org curid 470229

Sean Connery with members of the United States Air Force Reserve Band on Tartan Day

Of the millions of Scots over the centuries who have left the homeland to seek opportunities and better weather around the world, they have taken their names, traditions, education, culture and values with them.

This long and proud tradition of the Scots abroad has influenced a number of their adopted nations, including Argentina, Australia, Canada, Galicia, New Zealand, and the USA to celebrate Scotland with an annual Tartan Day.

3 In 1614, the Scottish mathematician John Napier invented a well-known mathematical instrument, the ingenious numbering rods more quaintly known as 'Napier's bones,' that offered mechanical means for facilitating computation.

Shapers

Scotland has been led and shaped by many people over the centuries. Four examples, relevant to the theme of this book are William Wallace, Robert the Bruce, James Douglas and Will-o'-Rule.

William Wallace 1272–1305–*Guardian of Scotland*

William Wallace was born in 1272, at Elderslie. Of noble descent, William's family is recorded as holding estates at Riccarton, Tarbolton, Auchinruive in Kyle and Stenton at Haddington. The Wallace families were vassals of James Stewart 5th, High Stewart of Scotland. William had two brothers, Malcolm and John. During his childhood, King Alexander the 3rd ruled Scotland in a time of peace and stability.

At eighteen years of age, William had grown up to be of great stature and strength. On one occasion while going through the streets of Lanark, he and some of his friends were set upon by Selbye, the son of the English Governor of Dundee and a few English soldiers. Wallace and his friends slew several of them and made their escape.

In 1286, while on his way to visit his wife on the Fife coast, King Alexander fell from his horse and died. His only heir to the Scottish throne was his granddaughter, Margaret, The Maid of Norway. Because she was a child, the Scottish lords decided on a government of guardians until she came of age. Margaret's death on her way from Norway to Scotland led to the period known as 'The Great Cause,' during which several men laid claim to the Scottish throne.

Civil war became a threat in Scotland, so to try and avoid this, the nobility approached King Edward of England to arbitrate. King

Edward jumped at the chance, having long wanted to unite Scotland with his kingdom of England.

There were four principal contenders, John Balliol, Robert Bruce, John Comyn, and William Ross. Seeing John Balliol as the weakest, Edward supported him and set about manipulating and grooming Balliol to his wishes.

John Balliol known derisively as 'Toom Tabard' (empty coat) was King of Scots from 1292 to 1296. In 1292, John Balliol, the elected, but morally weak Scottish arbitrator for King Edward of England, demanded that all Scottish lords and nobles should swear allegiance to King Edward. One individual, who would not yield to Edward, was William Wallace. He was subsequently classed as a traitor and an outlaw. This was one of the triggers of the long hard struggle for Scotland's independence.

By 1297, William had grown very strong and tall in stature. He married Marion, a lady from Lanark, who shortly after, was murdered by the Sheriff of Lanark, William de Heselrig, as a reprisal to William Wallace's exploits. In turn, William Wallace slew him.

Kenneth Turnbull

Statue of William Wallace
Wallace Monument, Stirling

One day when Wallace was fishing at Irvine, Earl Percy the Governor of Ayr, passed by with a number of English troops. Five of the troopers broke off and challenged Wallace for his fish. Wallace told them that they were welcome to half, but they demanded them all. Little did they know that their demands were about to cost them dearly—their lives. Wallace and his band of men then went into hiding in Ettrick Valley, not far from the town of Selkirk, located in the Scottish Borders.

Wallace made his encampment in the Ettrick Forest and with his men, went from there, engaging in many a fracas with small groups of English soldiers. Once he ventured in disguise into Ayr. An English man was boasting about how strong he was and was offering any Scot a groat (English silver coin worth four pennies) to strike him on his back with a pole as hard as they could.

Wallace offered the man three groats for a blow. The soldier was eager to accept. Wallace struck him a mighty blow and broke his back, whereupon the man fell to the ground and died. The man's comrades drew their swords and rushed at Wallace, who in turn, killed two of them with the pole and then drew his sword from under his long coat and fought his way out of Ayr. His reputation soon travelled around the Borders, and many young men flocked to join him in the Ettrick Forest. Through this, Wallace gained quite a large following.

The first battle of any great importance by Wallace and his men began when they attacked a 200 strong party of English soldiers carrying provisions from Carlisle to a garrison at Ayr. The commander was Sir John Fenwick, the man responsible for the death of Wallace's father.

The battle was long and desperate. Wallace killed Fenwick with his own hand. The English lost over 100 men before turning tail and fleeing for their lives. Several wagons of supplies and 200 carriages fell into the hands of Wallace and his men.

In September 1297, Wallace led a vastly outnumbered Scottish army to victory at the famous Battle of Stirling Bridge. He was subsequently knighted at Selkirk (Kirk of the Forest) and appointed Guardian of Scotland.

There are numerous stories of Wallace's guerrilla warfare in the west of Lanarkshire and Ayrshire.

Archie, the son of Sir William Forbes and Dame Mary Forbes, was growing up during Wallace's campaign. John Kerr, who had paid allegiance to King Edward, killed Archie's father and claimed his estate, Glen Cairn. Young Archie swore that someday he would avenge his father's death and reclaim his estate.

Like all other young males of his time, he was reared to have hate for the English and to give his life to restore Scotland's freedom. Until of age, these young lads knew no other game than training on the use of weaponry and the skill of battle. Archie and his pals practised their art with vigour every day. At 17 years of age, he was as skilful as any man in the art of combat.

William Wallace had become Archie's hero, and he vowed that one day he would join Wallace and fight in his cause. Archie was on a visit to Lanark one day when he heard the raised voices and clash of steel coming from a side street. Heading to see where it was coming from, he entered into a side street and came upon Wallace engaged in combat with five or six English soldiers. Seeing that Wallace was outnumbered, Archie drew his sword and joined in to help slay the Englishmen. The noise had attracted more English soldiers. Seeing this, Wallace and Archie prepared to make their escape and ran down the alleyway.

A woman stepped out from a doorway of one of the houses and motioned them inside. After they had entered, she barricaded the door and directed them to flee through the house and out the front door and made good their escape.

When they were a good way out of Lanark, Wallace stopped and asked Archie who he was. When Archie explained that he was the son of Sir William Forbes and the grandchild of Sir Richard Gordon, Wallace replied, 'I know well of your grandfather.' Wallace commended the skill with which Archie had demonstrated his exceptional swordsmanship.

When Wallace asked him what his intention was now, Archie said that he could no longer return home, as one of the men he had wounded was Sir John Kerr, and he now feared consequences. 'You had better come with me,' declared Wallace 'I could use a skilful swordsman like yourself.'

Archie had long dreamed of fighting alongside his hero.

A few days later, Wallace sent one of his scouts into Lanark to find out what news there may be of the woman who had helped them escape. The scout, on his return, informed Wallace of the fate of the woman. The sheriff of Lanark had her taken from her home and publicly executed. Archie saw the look of sheer anger and anguish on the face of Wallace. When asked who the woman was, Wallace replied, 'Her name was Marion. She was my wife.'

Wallace walked off a fair distance from the group that had gathered to hear the scout's report. After a few hours, he returned, and it was noted by his followers that there was a change in him by the features on his face, and by his unreserved declaration, 'This day will be greatly avenged.'

A few weeks earlier, Wallace had moved out of the Ettrick Valley, west of Lanarkshire, where he thought he would be best deployed to face resistance against the English. He made his headquarters on a shelf of rock on a craggy hill to the northeast and some nine miles from Lanark.

There was no shortage of stores and provisions as he had taken all they needed from the convoy that came from England to provide for the garrisons at Lanark and Ayr. Sometime after Wallace had grieved over the fate of his wife, he said to one of his lieutenants named, Grahame, 'I have done with grieving Grahame. It is now time for vengeance. Tonight, I will strike the first blow for the freedom of Scotland.'

William Wallace's sword

The English at this point had viewed Wallace as a tyrant and outlaw, but from now on it was to be full-scale war. Wallace declared to his band of men, 'Tonight, we will take Lanark.' With that, his followers shouted out with enthusiasm. A bugle sounded out loud and clear that echoed round the Lanarkshire hillsides.

Within two hours, a substantial force had gathered around Wallace. The party set off with torchbearers lighting the path that descended down from their high stronghold in the crags. At the foot, more men joined Wallace. To all who were to witness this attack on Lanark, they could be excused for thinking that this was an act of madness. Wallace's fighting strength was few compared to the 500 strong English garrison.

He halted his men about two miles from Lanark and issued his instructions. He ordered a tree to be felled and the removal of its branches. It was thirty feet in length and around two and a half feet in diameter. A rope was cut into short lengths while Wallace placed ten men on each side of the tree. The ropes were run under the tree trunk which was then lifted and carried by the men. As they approached the walls of Lanark, Wallace called for complete silence.

On entering the town, he divided his men into three groups. Sir John Grahame with one group and Sir Robert Thorne Auchinleck with another group, to arouse the town and attack any English soldiers they found in the street. Wallace himself, with Sir Archie Forbes, would attack the house of Hazelrig, the Governor of Lanark.

Wallace knew the town well and headed with his party to the moat, swam over and hauled himself up to the doorsill. He swung his heavy battle-axe and smote off the chains of the drawbridge, which in turn crashed down across the moat. The men carrying the tree trunk dashed across the drawbridge and soon battered down the heavy door. The Scots ran forward with the shout of, 'Death to the English and death to Hazelrig.'

The governor was long hated for the cruel onslaught that he had issued on the people of Lanark. With the English not knowing the size of Wallace's force, they were thrown into disarray and confusion.

The murder of Marion Bradfute (Wallace's wife) had also roused the indignation of the local people. A large number of the residents took up arms and fought the English in the streets.

When Wallace reached the door of Hazelrig's residence, he took his heavy axe and crashed the door to the floor. He grabbed Hazelrig by the throat, 'Villain!' he cried. Wallace and Forbes dragged him out into the street and called on everyone to come and witness his execution. Wallace backed off two paces, and with one mighty sweep of his axe, he removed Hazelrig's head from his body.

The aftermath had left 300 of the English garrison dead in the street with the rest fleeing for the English border. This action by Wallace helped to swell his army. Selkirk forest in the Borders was used by Wallace as his base for raiding and attacking Wishart's Palace at Ancrum. During the time Wallace spent in the Borders, he increased his army by recruiting members from border clans.

In 1297, King Edward issued orders for the Earl of Surrey to muster an army and march into the kingdom of central Scotland with a full-scale invasion. Their aim was to regain control of the rebellious Scots whom they regarded as their enemies.

Wallace set off from the Borders with his army and met up with Andrew Moray to join forces at Dundee early in September of that year. Moray, a very determined man, had led the Scottish independence uprising in north Scotland against the occupation of King Edward I.

Kenneth Turnbull

William Wallace Monument, Stirling

The following year, Wallace was involved in the Battle of Falkirk but was defeated. He resigned as Scotland's Guardian in favour of Robert The Bruce, the future king of Scotland, went into hiding, and made his way to France.

In 1304, Wallace returned to Scotland and became involved in more skirmishes. He knew that Scotland could not raise as big an army as King Edward, so he decided to examine the weakest points and strike where it hurt the most. He deployed what is known today as guerrilla warfare

In August 1305, Wallace, unable to evade capture, was betrayed and eventually tried for treason. He responded, 'I could not be a traitor to Edward, for I was never his subject.' Wallace was found guilty and executed on 23rd August at Smithfield in London. He was stripped naked and dragged through the city from Westminster to Smithfield. He was hung drawn and quartered. They then dismembered his body and impaled his head on London Bridge. His limbs were distributed to various parts of Britain; his right arm was sent to Newcastle, his left arm to Berwick on Tweed, his right foot to Perth and his left foot to Aberdeen.

King Robert the Bruce 1274–1329–*King of Scots*

Robert the Bruce, the 4th great-grandson of King David I and the grandson of Robert de Brus 5th, Lord of Annandale, had been a claimant to the throne of Scotland during the 'Great Cause,' following the death of King Alexander III and child queen Margaret. He is known as one of the greatest warriors and heroes of the nation and ultimately led Scotland to independence.

After killing his rival, John III (Red) Comyn, Robert seized the throne and was crowned King of Scots in March 1306. His forces being weaker than those of King Edward, King Robert was forced to flee and engage the English in his style of guerilla warfare. During this time, he defeated his Scottish rivals and won a number of skirmishes against the English. Gaining control of most of Scotland, he held his first parliament at St. Andrews in 1309.

Kenneth Turnbull

King Robert the Bruce

The Battle of Bannockburn was a defining time for King Robert, when in 1314 with a vastly outnumbered army, he cleverly used his local knowledge and unconventional tactics against a formidable English attack and decisively defeated them to re-establish the independence of his nation.

Despite his defeat at Bannockburn, Edward refused to recognise the independence of Scotland and sought support from the Scottish nobility. Instead, those nobles created the famous Declaration of Arbroath, declaring Robert as their king and Scotland as an independent kingdom. When his own people deposed Edward II, peace was made, and Scotland's independence was accepted by England with the Treaty of Edinburgh-Northampton in 1328.

Declaration of Arbroath - 1320

King Robert the Bruce died at his home in Cardross Castle in 1329. His body is buried in Dunfermline Abbey. His heart that was carried into battle by Sir James Douglas is interred at Melrose Abbey.

James Douglas 1289–1330–*Sir James the Good*

James, the eldest son of William Douglas (The Bold) was born in Lanarkshire, Scotland, around 1286. His mother died in childbirth and his father married Lady Eleanor De Ferres. She became the only mother James ever knew and he was very protective towards her.

In 1296, John Balliol the King of Scots repudiated his previous allegiance to King Edward of England who, in retaliation, invaded, beginning the Wars of Scottish Independence. John abdicated and the arms of Scotland were formally torn from his coat.

James, at the age of 10, witnessed the British attack on Berwick and the horrific consequences. James Douglas, along with his stepmother and two stepbrothers, were huddled together in a room in the lower part of Berwick Castle for three days whilst the fighting was going on. When the castle was surrendered, three English soldiers burst into the room in which Eleanor and the boys were hiding. One of the men, believed to be a commander, tried to rape Lady Eleanor who was with child. It is said that the young Douglas lunged at him with a knife his father had given him to protect his stepmother.

At the same moment, Lord Marmaduke entered the room and admonished the man who was trying to rape Eleanor. He ordered the three men to take her and the three boys to King Edward and left him to decide what to do with them. Lady Eleanor and the boys were taken up to the great hall and paraded in front of Longshanks, who was sitting on the dais. James's father was down on both knees in front of Longshanks. Edward said to him 'You are to blame for this Douglas, Richard of Cornwall, my nephew, is dead,' he lamented.

Edward paced up and down the hall and after some time he said to Douglas, 'What are the lives of your wife and sons worth and are you ready to swear your allegiance to me?' Lord Douglas, to save his family's lives, did swear fealty (his loyalty) to King Edward. He was then taken in chains and thrown into the dungeon of Berwick Castle. This was to be the last that young James Douglas would see his father for some time.

The next morning, Lady Eleanor and the three boys were put on an old cart and escorted out of Berwick to make the long journey back to Douglas Castle in Ayrshire. Thousands of bodies strewn along the sides of the road were a sight that the young James Douglas would never forget. He swore he would have revenge for his family and his fellow Scots against Longshanks and his English armies.

Kenneth Turnbull

Remains of Douglas Castle

In 1304, William Lamberton, the Bishop of St. Andrews, petitioned for the return of the Douglas ancestral lands to James, but this was rejected when Edward I realised whose son he was. The return of his ancestral lands became his personal crusade and a defining moment in the history of Scotland when he became the first noble supporter of William Wallace.

Douglas makes his feelings plain to Lamberton in 'The Brus' by John Barbour:

Sir, you see,
How the English tyrant forcibly
Has dispossessed me of my land
And you are made to understand
That the earl of Carrick claims to be
The rightful king of this country.
The English, since he slew that man,
Are keen to catch him if they can;
And they would seize his lands as well
And yet with him I faith would dwell!
Now, therefore, if it be your will,
With him will I take good or ill.
Through him, I hope my land to win
Despite the Clifford and his kin.

—John Barbour,
'The Brus'

James Douglas and other leaders of the Wars of Scottish Independence

William Brassey Hole CC SA 3.0

In 1306, Douglas made an alliance to join forces with Robert the Bruce and was soon recognised as a very clever military tactician. In the next year, he established his reputation on Palm Sunday in 1307, when he and his troops made a surprise attack on the English garrison. Some were killed in battle, and the rest were taken back to the castle, beheaded and thrown onto a fire.

Before leaving, he had the wells poisoned and razed the church to the ground, reclaimed his castle, destroyed all the provisions within it, and then razed it to the ground so that it was of no further use to the English. The locals regarded this gruesome attack as the 'Douglas Larder.' The English viewed James as 'The Blak Dowglas' as he was seen to be practising a psychological fear and guerrilla warfare.

James who served as Chief Commander in the Wars of Scottish Independence was honoured and fought as a knight banneret, leading a company of soldiers under his own banner for King Robert the Bruce on the fields of Bannockburn in 1314.

James Douglas brought great prestige to his clan. His family became one of the most powerful in Scotland and undoubtedly the most prominent in the Borders. Many Turnbulls fought under the banner of James Douglas.

As is described on the Bedrule Cairn, King Robert the Bruce granted Bedrule Castle to Sir James of Douglas, who entrusted its defence to the famous Rule Valley Turnbull reivers.

James was instrumental in taking back the town of Berwick on Tweed from the English in 1318, putting it back into Scottish hands for the first time since 1296.

When King Robert the Bruce was dying in 1329, he asked that Sir James Douglas, as his friend and lieutenant, should carry his heart to the Holy Land and present it at the Holy Sepulchre in Jerusalem.

Sir James Douglas was killed at the battle of Teba in Granada when his troops were ambushed, and valiantly he tried to rescue them but was outnumbered twenty to one. As a dying act, he defiantly threw the heart of King Robert the Bruce at the enemy, saying, 'Now pass thou onward as thou wert wont and Douglas will follow thee or die.'

His body and the casket with Bruce's heart were recovered. The heart is now interned in the Melrose Abbey cemetery.

The Scottish poet and chronicler, John Barbour, sums up with his poetic portrait of James Douglas (The Black Douglas).

But he was not so fair that we
Should praise his looks in high degree.
In visage he was rather grey;
His hair was black, so I heard say,
His limbs were finely made and long,
His bones were large, his shoulders strong,
His body was well-knit and slim
And those say that set eyes on him,
When happy, loveable was he,
And meek and sweet in company,
But those with him in battle saw
Another countenance he wore!

—John Barbour, 'The Brus'

Will-o'-Rule (The first Turnbull) c 1290–1333
Saved the Life of Robert the Bruce

William Rule, (Will- o'-Rule) was born towards the end of the 13th century to a modest family, most likely shepherds, in the Rule Valley near the village of Bedrule. He was a huge man for the day and said to be well over 6 feet tall. Because of his modest background, William Rule's legendary history is less well documented than for the other shapers reviewed here. This has led some to claim that he is mythical, but oral history and literary clues indicate otherwise.

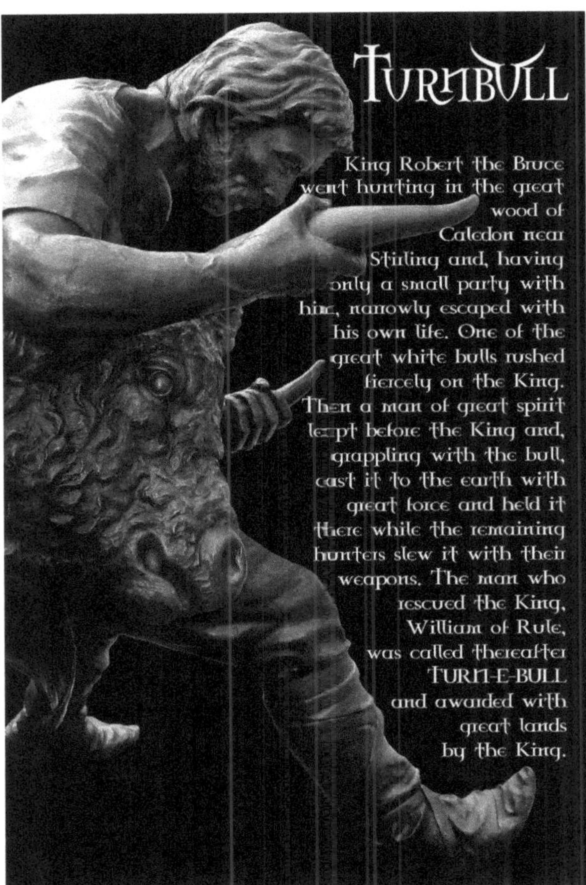

Hector Boece, Historian 1526

William added his strength to the forces of Robert the Bruce in the cause for Scottish independence. This was during the years following Bruce's being crowned King of Scots in 1306 and his victory for independence at the Battle of Bannockburn in 1314. During much of that time, Bruce's army was involved in guerrilla warfare and had to live off the land.

At the time the forest northwest of Stirling was known as Callendar, and it was here on a day in 1313 that Will-o'-Rule was part of a royal hunting party, and legend has it that the young man saved the life of Robert the Bruce. The king shot a wild bull with an arrow but did not kill it. The wounded beast charged Bruce and would have gored him but for the swift intervention of Will- o'-Rule, who grabbed the angry animal by the horns and turned the bull. According to different versions of the story, he either broke the animal's neck or held it down while the other hunters killed it with their swords. What is known is that the king dubbed him 'Turn-e-Bull.'

This story is recorded in the writings of Hector Boece, an early Scottish historian in his 'History of Scotland,' published in 1526. Reference to this story is recorded in the register of the Great Seal of Scotland. The poet, John Leyden *Scenes of Infancy: Descriptive of Teviotdale* includes his well-known description of the event.

Between red ezlar banks, that frightful scowl,
Fringed with grey hazel, roars the mining Roull;
here Turnbulls once, a race no power could awe,
Lined the rough skirts of stormy Rubers Law.
Bold was the chief, from whom their line they drew,
Whose nervous arm the furious Bison slew;
The Bison, fiercest race of Scotia's breed,
Whose bounding course outstripped the red deer's speed.
By hunters chafed, encircled on the plain,
He, frowning, shook his yellow lion-mane,
Spurned, with black hoof, in bursting rage, the ground,
And fiercely tossed his moony horns around.
On Scotia's lord, he rushed, with lightning speed,
Bent his strong neck, to toss the startled steed;
His arms robust the hardy hunter flung
Around his bending horns, and upward wrung,
With writhing force, his neck retorted round,
And rolled the panting monster on the ground,
Crushed, with enormous strength, his bony skull;
And courtiers hailed the man, who turned the bull.

—John Leyden, *Scenes of Infancy*

The wild cattle hunted in the forest were most likely not long-haired Highland cattle, but descendants of the large and fierce Bos primigenius, similar to the Pembroke cattle of today. From the skeletons preserved in Scotland's museums, the length of this gigantic Bos primigenius ox, averaged eleven to twelve feet and the shoulder height, about six feet.

The Pembroke cattle currently at Chillingham Castle in northern England closely resemble this Ox as described, in its essential structure. These cattle, although white in colour, are descendants of this Bos primigenius breed.

Kenneth Turnbull

Pembroke Bull

Edwin Landseer - 1867

Wild Cattle of Chillingham

For his act of bravery, Scotland's king not only changed William's name from Will-o-Roule to Turn-e-Bull, but also granted him lands at Philliphaugh, an area outside Selkirk, in the Borders. William Turn-e-Bull was to pay to the crown, 'one broad arrow on Assumption Day of the Virgin on the 15th of August each year.' William Turn-e-Bull took his family motto as 'I SAVED THE KING.' Eventually, the 'e' was dropped, and the name was written as 'Turnbull.' As the name increased in use, there have been variations of its spelling over time.

Scottish history could well have been very different if it had not been for the bravery of Will-o-Roule. The Turnbull name was held with great pride, not only because of its origin but because surnames themselves had only become common during the previous century and during the reign of King William, who was then known as 'The Lion of Scotland.'

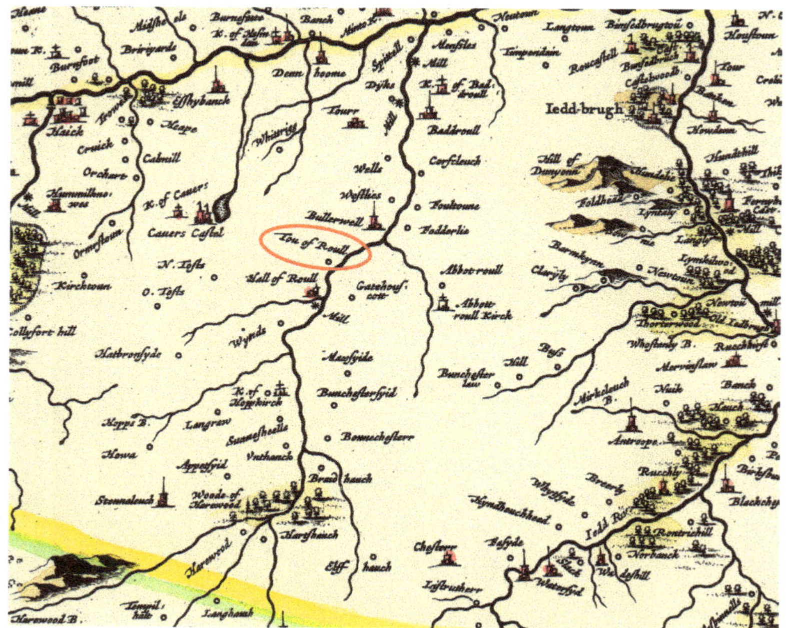

A section of an old 1600's map of the Borders showing
Town o' Rule (Tou of Roull)

Kenneth Turnbull

A small section of the old Callendar Forest, overlooking what would have been part of the Jedforest in earlier times. The Scots Pines, as seen here, are amongst the species that existed at the time of the Royal hunting encounter.

Tales

Battles

Sir Edward Coley Burne-Jones (1882)

The kings of England held a desire to be overlords of the whole island of Britain. In addition, there were inevitable territorial disputes between England and Scotland over the so-called Debatable Lands along the border.

At times, Welsh princes and Scottish kings accepted the English claim, as long as they were left alone within their own territories. For centuries, the border was constantly being altered and strategic border strongholds, particularly Carlisle, Berwick-upon-Tweed, and the now-vanished town of Roxburgh, changed hands back and forth between the two kingdoms. With this continual unrest, which lasted about 300 years, the resulting conflicts and battles brought out the best and the worst of all concerned, both within the clans and on either side of the border.

A number of those conflicts are described in this text, chosen as examples of both large and small battles, including victories for both sides. The following list, which is far from complete, primarily includes conflicts in and near the Borders.

The 1200's

Alexander III–1241-1286

Alexander III ended the Norse threat when he defeated an invasion force led by the Norwegian king, Haakon IV, at the battle of Largs in 1263. Peace with both the Vikings and England was further cemented in 1281 by the marriage of Alexander's daughter, Margaret, to Norway's King Eric II.

Kim Traynor - CC SA 3.0

Statue of Alexander III St. Giles, Edinburgh

The period of relatively good relations between England and Scotland ended with two events towards the end of the 13th century; the accessions of Edward I (Hammer of the Scots) to the English throne in 1272 and the death of Alexander III in 1286. The new English king, strong-willed and warlike, was determined to more actively assert the claim of his predecessors to lordship over all of Britain.

Edward conquered Wales, encircling it with mighty fortresses. With the death of the Scottish king, he saw an opportunity to intervene in the affairs of the Scottish crown. This began the Wars of Scottish Independence.

The First War began in 1296 and ended with the signing of the Treaty of Edinburgh-Northampton in 1328. The Second War began in 1332 and ended in 1357 with the signing of the Treaty of Berwick. At the end of both wars, Scotland successfully remained independent.

Sacking of Berwick on Tweed–1296

When John Balliol (King of Scots, 1292-1296) was deposed by Scottish nobles in 1296, King Edward invaded Scotland, thus invoking the Wars of Scottish Independence. He advanced on the Scots with a large army to the town of Berwick on Tweed, which is located 2½ miles south of the current Scottish border at the mouth of the River Tweed. Berwick, the largest town in Scotland at that time, had a population of around 18,000 inhabitants.

King Edward I (Longshanks) appeared before the town of Berwick on the morning of Friday the 30th March in 1296. King Edward's men easily breached the walls of the town, and a horrific slaughter began. For three days the English killed anyone they found, regardless of age or sex. It is said that over 15,000 lives were lost in this brutal slaughter.

Only when King Edward saw a woman in the act of childbirth being dragged from her house and savagely butchered by one of his soldiers, did he call off his men. The sacking (destruction) of Berwick was to become a considerable stain on English history and a warning of what English involvement could mean to the Scots.

Battle of Stirling Bridge–1297

Sir William Wallace and Sir Archie Forbes fought as one in many affrays throughout the Borderlands and attacked supplies being conveyed to English garrisons in Lanark, Ayr and Stirling. Wallace's most significant victory over the English has to be the Battle of Stirling Bridge, fought on the 11th September 1297, during the first major war of Scottish independence.

News had reached Wallace that a large English force had set out from Berwick and was advancing on Stirling. When word reached him of the English advance, Wallace was besieging the castle at Dundee. Wallace sent word to Sir Archie Forbes and to Sir Andrew Moray, a great friend, to join him at Stirling. It was essential for Wallace to gather together as many Scots capable of bearing arms as possible.

The English Earl of Surrey, Hugh de Cressingham, led an army of 50,000 on foot and 1,000 on horse, while Earl Percy advanced from Carlisle with 8,000 strong on foot and 300 horses. Wallace left Sir Alexander Scrymgeour, to carry on the siege at Dundee and headed for Stirling to defend the only bridge on which King Edward's army could cross the River Forth to Stirling.

Unknown artist

The Battle of Stirling Bridge 1297

The Earl of Surrey, thus far, had received no resistance as he advanced with such a large force and felt secure of a successful assault. A large part of his army was made up of veterans who had fought in the wars at home, in Wales, and against the French. By contrast, Wallace's troops with no real military training were made up of men who were solely opposed to English rule. They were rudely armed and with little experience in facing such a large force.

Wallace assembled his troops on high ground north of the forth, where they were protected from observation by the high hills behind Cambuskenneth Abbey, known as Abbey Craig. At a bend in the river, opposite the craig, was the bridge by which the English army would have to cross. Wallace and Sir Archie Forbes stood on top of the craig watching the English approach. It must have been a frightening sight for those two brave men to look down on such a large enemy encampment with its pavilions, banners, and pennons lying in the valley and within sight of the old castle rising in the background. This prospect would have brought fear into the hearts of the fainthearted when compared to the size of Wallace's force.

One could be forgiven for thinking that it would be suicidal to engage in a battle with such great odds, true Scots and brave men as they were. Three days prior to the battle, the Steward of Scotland, the Earl of Lennox, and other magnates entered Surrey's camp to beg him not to attack until they tried to induce the people to lay down their arms. They returned saying that the Earl of Surrey was not prepared to listen.

When the nobles left Wallace's encampment to return home, they encountered some English soldiers. A fight broke out, resulting in one of the English soldiers being wounded by the Earl of Lennox. News of this reached the Earl of Surrey, so he decided to wait no longer and gave the order to start the assault the following morning.

At daybreak, on the morning of the 11th September, Wallace was awakened with the news that the English were crossing the bridge. His troops were eager to rush down and commence battle, but Wallace restrained them.

Around 5,000 Welsh foot soldiers crossed the bridge. Then, unexpectedly there was a pause. No one was seen to follow. Wallace stood his ground to wait until half of the Earl of Surrey's men had crossed. The number of Scots under William Wallace's command is not known, but the majority of estimates place it below 20,000 and as an English historian, who best describes the battle, said of it as the 'defeat of many by the few.'

The Earl of Surrey's contempt for the Scots had undoubtedly clouded his judgment in his attempt to engage in such a position. The bridge was only wide enough for two or three horsemen to cross abreast and when those who had passed were attacked, assistance could not reach them from the rear. The English knights and men-at-arms, with the Royal standard and the Earl of Surrey's banner, crossed first, followed by the infantry.

William Wallace held his troops until half the English army had crossed the bridge, then he gave the order to charge. Sir Andrew Moray, with 2,000 men, descended upon them from the hill on the right. On seeing this, the English cavalry charged against them. The instant they did so, Wallace, with his main army, charged down from the craig and swept away the English near the head of the bridge. This manoeuver caused the whole of the English infantry, who had crossed, to be cut off from any assistance as they were forced to watch from the far bank. The narrowness of the bridge made any move to reinforce those unfortunates impossible.

The English men-at-arms succeeded in overthrowing the Scot's infantry when they had charged and pursued them for some distance. Upon turning back to rejoin, they saw that the situation had changed drastically. The troops that were left at the head of the bridge had been overthrown and destroyed. The Royal standard and the banner of Surrey was down and the bridge in the possession of the Scots. The men-at-arms charged back to try to recover the bridge, but it was all in vain.

The Scots fought on bravely. Those in front made a hedge of pikes, while those behind hurled darts and poured showers of arrows, killing the men-at-arms. Many perished trying to swim back over the river. Only one gained the other side. Wallace and his men joined those attacking the English and Welsh who had been cornered in the premonitory of the river.

Wallace and Moray had, as part of their force, blocked the northern end of the bridge. What the larger part of the English army saw was horrifying. The Scots in the rush down from the Abbey Craig would have gathered an immense momentum. This must have driven many of the English off the bank and into the river. Those who escaped this fate cannot have had time to offer any significant opposition. Their superior weapons could not be brought to bear in the crush. Retreat was impossible. The Scots made a great slaughter of the vanguard. A hundred knights and many infantry, perhaps as many 5,000, died, either killed or drowned.

Among those who perished was Hugh de Cressingham, son of Henry III and treasurer of the English Administration in Scotland. The Earl of Surrey had not crossed the bridge, but the treasurer had been less prudent. He had charged at the head of the vanguard, his mind no doubt filled with the dreams of that glory which the office of treasurer had denied him. Misguided, pompous, and less than popular with his own army, he met the same cruel end he was known to have provided Scottish prisoners of war. He was dragged down from his horse and died under the spears of the Scots infantry.

Janfrie - CC SA 3.0

Stirling Bridge with Wallace Monument in background

In telling of his death, Walter of Guisborough in his *Chronicle* of English history does not spare him, 'Of all the many who were deceived that day, he was deceived most of all.' After the battle, the Scots, in a gruesome ceremony, flayed his obese body. Strips of his skin were sent throughout Scotland to proclaim the victory of Stirling. Wallace himself had a baldrick belt made for his sword from what was left of Cressingham's skin.

Of those who escaped from the massacre, some swam the river. These were Welshmen who fought as always, without armour. The most famous of those who did survive, was Sir Marmaduke De Tweng of Yorkshire. He refused to join the Welshmen as they swam the river and managed to ride his horse through the Scots and over the bridge to safety. He, clearly, had seen the hopelessness of the situation very early when the bridge was still intact.

Sir Marmaduke De Tweng's courage and his continued devotion to the English Crown, first in the person of Edward I and then in that of the king's son, ensured that his reputation did not suffer. The same could not be said of the Earl of Surrey. He gave Stirling Castle over to Sir Marmaduke De Tweng's keeping and fled for Berwick with unseemly haste.

Flushed with success, the Scots were unstoppable. When Wallace saw that this quarter was secure, he led a large number of followers across the bridge where the English still outnumbered the Scots. The sight however of the terrible devastation that had befallen half their number, had utterly demoralised them and when they saw the Scots cross the bridge, they fled in terror.

Hot pursuit was kept up, and a great number of the English army was slain. More than 20,000 English perished in the battle. The remainder crossed the border as broken fugitives. The Earl of Surrey who had fled the battlefield managed to reach Dunbar Castle, where he boarded a ship for England.

After this great victory by Wallace, the people of Scotland made Wallace and Moray the Keepers of Scotland. Unfortunately, Moray was to die soon after from wounds he received in the battle.

Battle of Falkirk–1298

On 22nd July 1298, an English army arrived at Falkirk to face Wallace. The English army had marched into Edinburgh on the 1st of April, pillaged the Lothian area and gained a few strongholds.

The Scots army of 6,000 was composed mostly of spearmen arranged in four schiltrons. Their great pikes pointed outwards, gave the formations a formidable appearance. Between the schiltrons were archers and at the back, knights and swordsmen led by John Comyn.

The English army of 15,000 included 2,500 cavalry formed into four battalions, with one commanded by the king himself. Behind them were thousands of archers and spearmen.

The Scottish cavalry charged the English, but seeing the vast numbers that were formed against them, the party of men-at-arms under John Comyn fled the field immediately, abandoning their fellow Scottish comrades to the slaughter.

Edward's Welsh longbowmen moved up and quickly overcame the smaller number of Scottish archers. The schiltrons of spearmen with their pikes became an easy target as they had no shields and nowhere to hide. The battle was lost for Wallace and his men almost as soon as the first arrows began to fall.

Around 2,000 were killed on either side, but that represented a third of the Scottish troops in the battle. The survivors, including William Wallace, escaped into the nearby forest of Torwood.

Wallace was badly defeated. He made good his escape but received the blame in spite of the desertion by Comyn and the other nobles. In September of the same year, Wallace resigned his guardianship of Scotland to the Earl of Carrick (Robert The Bruce), the future king of Scotland.

The 1300's

The Battle of Bannockburn–1314

In 1306, King Robert the Bruce seized control of the throne and tensions between Scotland and England rose once more. The following year, Edward II became heir to the English throne, but he was incapable of the leadership shown by his father.

Stirling Castle had become a vital stronghold held by the English because it was the gateway to the Highlands. In 1314, King Robert the Bruce's brother, Edward, laid siege to the castle and negotiaed an agreement that if the castle was not relieved with fresh troops by mid-summer, then it would be surrendered back to the Scots. The English had agreed and began to organise themselves for a major campaign to break the siege.

The Scottish army consisted of between 7,000 and 10,000 strong, while the English had 2,000 cavalry and 15,000 infantry and many of them as longbowmen. The Scottish cavalry were also reputed to have had around 500 light horsemen. The English forces were around twice the size of the Scottish troops.

Edmund Bleigh, Leighton (1909)

Bruce addresses troops before the Battle of Bannockburn

Edward II had ideas where his forces were likely to be challenged and sent his troops north to attack in four divisions toward the River Forth near Stirling. The Scots, by contrast, had three divisions known as 'sheltrons' (shiltrons) where each division was made up of strong defensive circles of men bristling with long pikes.

Thomas Randolf, the Earl of Moray, was the commander of the Scottish frontline and King Robert the Bruce commanded the rearguard. His brother, Edward, led the third division. According to historians, there was also a fourth division under the command of James Douglas.

Most medieval battles lasted only a few hours, but this was to last two days.

On the 23rd June, the English forces advanced, commanded by the Earls of Gloucester and Hereford and encountered a division of Scots, among them King Robert the Bruce himself. One mounted English knight, Henry de Broun, charged King Robert, engaging him in single combat. When the two horses passed side by side,

Bruce split Bohun's head with his axe and killed him. The Scots division in tight formation then charged with their extended pikes and pushed back the English.

In the evening, the English crossed the stream known as the Bannock Burn and camped overnight. This was just as King Robert the Bruce had hoped they would do. Scottish knight, Alexander Sexton, who deserted the English camp and encouraged King Robert to attack had informed him that the morale of the English was low.

Not long after daybreak, on the second day, the Scots spearmen advanced on the open field. Edward II witnessed the Scots advancing but was surprised when they stopped and knelt in prayer. He misread this and is thought to have said, 'They pray for mercy!' But, they were praying for God's mercy, that they would be victorious or die.

The Earl of Gloucester led a charge despite the Earl of Hereford arguing that the battle should be postponed. Not to be seen as a coward, he was perhaps goaded into the charge through this. However, few of his men accompanied him, and when he reached the Scottish lines, he was surrounded and killed. Added to this, the Scots slowly advanced with their shiltron formation attack and pushed the English back. The English attempted to counter with longbows, but were causing casualties on their own and ceased fire.

The English were hemmed in through the 'U' shaped stream that lay behind them, making it difficult to manoeuvre. With this confronting them, the English broke ranks and fled. King Edward II also decided to flee with his bodyguard. With no one to give them orders, panic set in and the English defeat turned into a rout. Many tried to reach the English border 90 miles away, but countless more were killed, either through injuries or by drowning.

Of their English army of 17,000, only 5,000 escaped. Another 500 were spared and held as hostages for ransom. By contrast, the Scottish casualties were surprisingly very light, with only two knights among those who were killed.

In the struggles for Scottish independence, the battle of Bannockburn was a significant and major victory. In effect, it was a historical turning point for Scotland, that brought independence and peace to the Borders, but only for a time, as the victory opened up the Borders for raids on the English.

The Comyns were as much the losers at Bannockburn as the English. Bruce's actions between the years of 1306-1314, ultimately led to the demise of the Comyn family in Scottish politics and any claim they might have wished to the crown of Scotland.

Treaty of Edinburgh-Northampton–1328

On the 17th March 1328, a peace treaty between the kingdoms of England and Scotland was signed in Edinburgh by Robert the Bruce, King of Scotland, and ratified by the English Parliament at Northampton on the 1st May. This treaty brought an end to the First War of Scottish Independence, which had begun when the English invaded Scotland in 1296. The treaty document, written in French, is now held by the National Archives of Scotland.

According to the terms of the treaty, England recognised Scotland as a fully independent nation, with Robert the Bruce and his successors as its rightful rulers. The treaty also defined the border between Scotland and England.

However, the treaty recognising Scottish independence did not end the conflict. Even when the two kingdoms were technically at peace, local warfare continued to rage between the landowners on both sides of the border.

These powerful landowners, largely independent of royal control from either London or Edinburgh, were able to do pretty much what they wanted in the remote and warlike Borders lands.

One of the greatest and longest-running feuds was between the English Percy family and the Scottish Douglas family, both of whom laid claim to a significant portion of the Debatable Lands. Because of their loyalty to Sir James Douglas, the Turnbulls were involved in many battles on both sides of the border during this period.

Battle of Halidon Hill–1333

The border town of Berwick-upon-Tweed has seen many sieges throughout its history when the town changed hands between

England and Scotland fourteen times (more than any other town) until finally remaining with the English in 1482. The great siege of 1333 was one of the longest, lasting three months.

After Robert the Bruce's decisive victory over Edward II of England at Bannockburn in 1314, Scottish independence was safe until Bruce's death in 1329, when the familiar problems reappeared.

Bruce's successor, David II was only five years old and Edward Balliol, son of John Balliol who had ruled Scotland during the 1290's as an English puppet, returned from exile with an army. He was crowned King of Scotland in 1332 but was soon ousted by Sir Archibald Douglas and the Earl of Moray. Balliol withdrew to the Borders, where he sought help from King Edward III. Naturally, the English king was only too delighted to assist.

In March 1333, Edward Balliol laid siege to Berwick, which at that time, was in Scottish hands. After about two months, King Edward III and an English army joined him, and in May, the siege of Berwick began in earnest. Among the techniques used by the besiegers was an early form of biological warfare that was comprised by catapulting severed heads into the town in order to spread disease.

After nearly two months, Berwick's defences were crumbling, and both besiegers and defenders were becoming frustrated. An agreement was made that there would be a truce and that if Berwick were not relieved within 15 days of the 11th July, the town would surrender to the English. This truce was guaranteed by the holding of twelve hostages including the two young sons of Sir Alexander Seaton, the Deputy Commander of the town.

Scottish hopes depended on the arrival of reinforcements led by Sir Archibald Douglas, who managed to send some supplies into the town, but Edward III did not consider this sufficient to qualify as relieving it. To lure the besiegers away, Douglas threatened to march south and pillage northern England.

King Edward III called Douglas's bluff. Gallows were erected as close to the walls of Berwick as possible and some of the hostages, including the two young Seaton boys, were hanged. A new and somewhat confusing agreement followed. There would be a further truce until 20th July and Berwick would surrender to the English if not relieved by then.

The failure of Sir Archibald Douglas to draw the English army from Berwick by attacking Bamburgh resulted in a crushing defeat at the Battle of Hallidon Hill on the 19th July, which sealed the town's fate. Before the battle commenced, Will-o'-Rule Turnbull stepped out of the Scottish ranks and challenged the English knights to a duel.

Igor Adasikov - Taimy Studios

The duel at Halidon Hill

Will-o'-Rule had a mastiff hound that followed him into battle. As the story goes, when Will-o'-Rule challenged the English knight Sir Robert Benhale to combat, the mastiff hound attacked first and was severed in two by a mighty swipe of the knight's sword. In the single combat that followed, Turnbull lost an arm and then his head.

The English had the better position, but the English army had been weakened by desertions. Edward divided his army into three divisions. While he commanded the centre, Sir Edward Bohun led the right wing, and Edward Balliol led the left wing. The Scots were also organised into three divisions, led by the Earl of Moray, Robert the Stewart and Sir Archibald Douglas.

As the Scots advanced across the marshy ground at the base of the hill, their horses became bogged down, so the cavalry troops had to dismount and thus became sitting targets for the English and Welsh archers. Wave after wave of arrows descended on the slow-moving Scottish soldiers. The ensuing English cavalry charge swept them from the field of battle that decisively led to a slaughter. One of the casualties was Douglas himself.

The next day, Berwick surrendered to the English and Edward Balliol was reinstated as King of Scotland. Young David II went into exile in France for safety. As a puppet ruler, Balliol ceded Scottish territory to England, which hardly endeared him to his subjects.

In spite of their heavy losses, the Turnbulls and other Borders clans were not intimidated and continued to support the return of David II as the rightful King of Scotland.

Battle of Neville's Cross–1346

Jean Froissart 14th century

The unpopular Edward Balliol was driven into exile, and King David II returned to Scotland in 1341. King Edward III was heavily engaged in the Hundred Years War with France.

In 1346, the English army inflicted a crushing defeat on the French at Crecy. In the same year, King David II invaded England in response to a request for assistance from his French ally, Philip VI.

The Turnbulls, Elliots, Armstrongs, and other border clans marched with the Scottish army on Durham in northeast England. They camped in the Bearpark, an estate belonging to the priors of Durham just to the west of the city.

Meanwhile, in the absence of both Edward III and the Prince-Bishop of Durham off in France, the Archbishop of York, together with politicians Ralph Neville and Henry Percy, hastily gathered together an English army at Bishop Auckland.

The armies met at Neville's Cross, named after an ancient preaching cross just one mile to the west of Durham. It is alleged that after the battle, Ralph Neville (the names are purely coincidental) had a new cross erected in commemoration of the victory.

The English army assembled on the ridge of Red Hill, and the Scots lined up a little to the north on Crossgate Moor. To the east was the steep wooded ravine of Flass Vale (then a bog) and to the west, the valley of the river Browney. The Scots had a numerical advantage, numbering around 16,000 men, while the English, severely depleted because of the war in France, could scarcely muster 5,000.

As the Scots advanced across the moor towards their opponents, the English archers repeatedly mowed them down. Wave after wave of attacks were halted with heavy losses.

The Scots were pushed back, and those who remained on the field of battle were encircled. A series of subsequent charges by the English cavalry eventually won the day. It was during the final stages of the battle that King David II was wounded and captured. As they tried to escape the carnage, the Scottish soldiers were hampered by the terrain, and either drowned as they swam across the River Browney or slowed down as they tried to cross Flass Vale bog.

BabelStone - CC SA 3.0

Odiham Castle in Hampshire where David II was imprisoned from 1346 to 1357

After his defeat and capture, the Scottish King David II spent the next eleven years in captivity in England. He was released and restored to the Scottish throne in 1357, following the payment of a ransom of 100,000 marks which equates to approximately £20 million today.

Battle of Otterburn–1388

Very few Borders battles have been recorded without one or more of the Turnbulls being implicated, and indeed, when the occasion arose, the whole of the clan rallied to Sir James Douglas to defend their homeland or attack the 'auld enemy' over the Border.

The battle of Otterburn on the 19th August 1388, was one of the classic conflicts in the long feud between two of the most powerful of the Borders families, the Percys on the English side and the Douglases on the Scottish side. Taking advantage of the fact that the English King Richard II was a minor, James, 2nd Earl of Douglas led around 3,000 men on a raid into England in 1388.

The Scots pillaged and burned Durham but were held by an English army led by the Percys, Henry (Hotspur) and his brother Ralph, in a skirmish outside Newcastle. During the skirmish, Douglas captured Hotspur's lance pennon and taunted him to recover it. For medieval knights, this was a matter of honour and a challenge that Hotspur could not ignore.

L. Pennell Border Antiquities - 1814

The lance pennon taken by Douglas from the English knight, Hotspur

In spite of his personal victory over Percy, Douglas found the city too well fortified and led his men back towards Scotland. Humiliated and angry, Percy gathered his troops and set out to attack the Scots who were by then, encamped 30 miles away near Otterburn Castle. Rather than wait to attack the next day, Percy decided to attack by the light of the moon, thinking that his victory would be assured, as he had almost three times as many soldiers as Douglas.

Being tired from the long march and because Percy's tactics were rash, the English suffered a great defeat. Sir Henry Percy, his brother Sir Ralph Percy, and many other English knights were taken prisoner. Records indicate that 1,040 English were captured and 1,860 killed, compared with 200 Scots captured and 100 killed. Sir James Douglas was killed during the battle, and his body was taken back for burial at Melrose Abbey.

The decisive outcome and the death of James Douglas kept the two sides apart for over ten years. As a result of the battle of Otterburn, several ballads were composed in its honour including 'The Battle of Otterburn' and The Ballad of 'Chevy Chase.' Though the details of those ballads are not historically accurate, 'Chevy Chase' is known to be one of the best ancient ballads.

The 1500's

Battle of Flodden–1513

Stephen McKay - CC BSA 2.0

Flodden Memorial

When Henry VIII invaded France in May 1513, James IV invaded England in support of Louis XII of France, according to the terms of the Auld Alliance. This led to the Battle of Flodden Field, also known as Branxton Moor, in September of that same year. In terms of numbers of troops, this was the largest battle ever fought between the two nations. The result was a decisive English victory.

On the morning of the 9th September 1513, the Earl of Surrey, heading an army of 26,000 men, advanced through the bleak countryside of Northumberland on his way to face the Scots on Flodden Moor. The sheer scale of such an intrusion, with the noise of the clanging armour, wagons, sheep, goats, cattle and the long unruly trail of camp followers, would have been unnerving to the people of the countryside.

From the banks of the River Till, the English faced a four-mile march to Branxton Ridge. After the first three miles, they descended into the shallow valley of the Pallinsburn, a minor obstacle, but it was swollen by heavy rain and had become a spongy mire. Branxton Ridge sloped upwards for 300 ft with a reverse slope up towards the lower crest of Pipers Hill, where the present monument stands.

Whilst the vanguard filed over the bridge the guns had to be left with

Surrey's division, crossing by the ford, as the planks were incapable of bearing their great weight.

King James VI's Scottish army at this time was unaware of the enemy's intention. The English were nowhere to be seen, so it appeared to the king that the honours might be his. By early afternoon scouts were reporting movement west of the River Till, and though at first he refused to believe it, James was forced to realise that he was outflanked. Calling for his horse, the king rode out to see for himself. There could be no doubt that the English were coming.

The combat was particularly savage and the slaughter was terrible. The English fought with the cold fury of men who began the day thinking themselves as being under the threat of death. Robert V, Lord Maxwell and William III, Lord Herries, were amongst the first Scottish peers to fall and on the English side, Sir John Gower and Sir Richard Harbottle.

The fighting in the centre began around 4:30 pm and lasted for two long, bloody, and exhausting hours. At some point, Bothwell committed the reserve division, but ineptly, so that his men crowded the rear of the king's division rather than attacking the flank where they might have had an effect.

The result was a decisive English victory. The injured were taken down to the little church in Branxton Village. In the churchyard, there can still be found graves where some of the dead are buried. King James IV of Scotland was amongst those who were killed, making him the last monarch in the British Isles to die in battle.

Battle of Sclaterford–1513

Another skirmish, which took place on Turnbull lands, was the Battle of Sclaterford. Following the defeat of the Scottish army at Flodden Field, Lord Dacre led a 5,400 strong English army north to plunder the Borders. It was the heroism of one George Turnbull who rallied 700 Turnbulls along with the Douglases, Scotts, Rutherfords, and Kerrs to defeat the invaders in the Rule Valley. Lord Dacre's report to King Henry VIII said 'and so went to Sclaterford on the water of Bowset, and there the Scots pursued us right sore. There bickered with us, and gave us hand strokes.'

Kenneth Turnbull

Plaque on Fodderlee bridge that spans the Bowset (also called Fodderlee bum) near the junction of the Bowset and the Rule

Hornshole Skirmish–1514

Hornshole, in the Scottish Borders, is just two miles outside Hawick. The crushing defeat for Scots the previous year at the Battle of Flodden, had wiped out most of the able-bodied men of the Borders.

The English, knowing the vulnerability of the Scots, invaded. Their marauders wreaked havoc on the defenceless border towns. Leaving famine and destruction behind them, they burned towns and houses, stole cattle and sheep, and destroyed crops.

Unknown - 1800's

Hornshole Bridge

On a night in 1514, word came to the citizens of Hawick that a band of English raiders had set up camp and posted sentries at Hornshole. Many people of Hawick scattered to the hills, but a number of young men (callants) gathered together to save their beloved home.

Using makeshift weapons, they circled around the campsite of the English raiders in the dark of the night. The English, sleepy and drunk, never knew what hit them.

The lads gathered the livestock and horses and rushed into camp, crying out, 'Teribys!' their ancient war cry. Beneath the hooves of the stampeding cattle and horses, most never had a chance to wake and defend themselves. The callants were not only able to defeat the English threat they also captured the battle standard of their enemy and rode proudly back into town waving their trophy in defiance. Hawick's coat of arms includes a pennon inscribed with 1514, in commemoration of this brave deed. Border ridings became known as 'Common Ridings.' Each year since 1703, except for the two World Wars, Hawick selects a Calant to commemorate this historic event from more than 500 years ago.

Kenneth Turnbull

Memorial Ridings statue in the main street of Hawick

Battle of Solway Moss–1542

The Solway Moss battle was the culmination of many years of fighting between the Scottish and English kings in the Debatable Lands. It all came to a head when King Henry VIII asked his nephew, King James V of Scotland to break away from the Roman Catholic Church. When the Scottish king rejected his request, Henry VIII was furious at his nephew's response and sent his troops into Scotland.

King James V retaliated by having Robert Lord Maxwell raise an army, and on the 24th of November, the Scots sent an army of 15,000-18,000 of disorganised and poorly led troops into England. Lord Maxwell said he would personally lead the attack, but this became a problem when several of the others refused to accept his command.

The British Commander, Lord Wharton and his army met the Scots at Solway Moss, located on the English side of the Anglo-Scottish Borders near the River Esk. The Scots found themselves penned in between the river and the Moss peat bog. After intense fighting, the Scots were defeated and surrendered to the English cavalry.

Andrew Smith - CC SA 2.0

River Esk - Battle of Solway Moss site

Several hundred Scots in their attempts to escape, were drowned in the marshes and around 1,200 were also taken prisoner. The English released a number of earls and lairds, with 'pledges' (hostages) sent to England in their place. The English intent was that when the prisoners returned to Scotland, they would further the English cause. However, the Scottish government would not allow some of the prisoners back over the border and regarded them as traitors for their loss in the battle at Solway Moss.

King James V, who had not been at the scene of the battle, was bitterly disappointed when he heard the result and felt dishonoured with the loss of his banner. He was ill with a fever and withdrew to Falkland Palace at Fife. Added to this and with hopes for a newborn son, he learned that his wife had just delivered a daughter. Two weeks later at the age of thirty, he died.

Battle of Pinkie Cleugh–1547

The Battle of Pinkie Cleugh, took place on 10th September 1547, at Musselburgh on the banks of the River Esk, approximately 7 miles east of Edinburgh.

It was thirty years after the Battle of Flodden and tensions again rose between England and Scotland. In July 1543, following the death of her father, when Mary, Queen of Scots was only six weeks old, the Treaty of Greenwich was signed. The agreement provided for the marriage of Henry VIII's son, Edward VI, to Mary when she reached the age of 10. As the last legitimate child of King James V of Scotland, Mary had become his heir to the throne.

Through King Henry VIII's diplomatic plan, he aimed to secure an alliance between Scotland and England. But, this was to end in failure, as the Treaty of Greenwich, was rejected by the Scottish Parliament in December of that same year.

Frustrated by the rejection, Henry VIII launched an attack against Scotland, known as the 'War of Rough Wooing' in an attempt to force the marriage to take place. The war lasted eight years and ultimately led to the Battle of Pinkie Cleugh.

The war that ensued also had a religious aspect. The Church of England was established when the English broke away from the authority of the state church of the Roman Empire in the 1530's.

The Scots refused to have the Church of England forced upon them, as the Roman Catholic Church had been firmly established in Scotland for nearly a thousand years. The English influence included supplying Protestant literature in the Lowlands of Scotland when they invaded.

King Henry VIII died in 1547, so Edward Seymour, his maternal uncle, became Lord Protector and Duke of Somerset. He continued the policy of seeking an alliance with Scotland by the marriage of Mary to Edward and imposing an Anglican Reformation on the Scottish Church.

The Duke of Somerset moved quickly and invaded with his well-equipped army, supported by a massive naval fleet. They approached along the east coast but were constantly harassed by the Scottish Border reivers.

To oppose their advance, the Earl of Arran had collected a large army, consisting mainly of pikemen (soldiers on foot with long pointed poles) with contingents of archers from the Highlands. He also had many cannons, but these were not as mobile as Somerset's. Arran occupied the west bank slopes of the River Esk to slow Somerset's advance. The Firth of Forth was on his left flank, and a large bog protected his right. Some fortifications were constructed where a cannon and arquebuses (hook guns and forerunners to the rifle) were mounted. Some of these guns pointed out into the forth to keep the English warships at a distance.

Early on Saturday, 10th September 1547, the Duke of Somerset advanced his army to close up with another detachment at Inveresk.

He found that the Earl of Arran had moved his army across the Esk River via the Roman bridge and was advancing rapidly to meet him. The Earl of Arran knew himself to be outmatched in artillery, so he tried to force close combat before the English artillery could deploy. During the battle, the Scots taunted the English soldiers as 'loons,' 'tykes,' and 'heretics.'

Kim Traynor - CC SA 3.0

Roman bridge across the Esk River in Musselburgh

On the other flank, the Duke of Somerset threw in his cavalry to delay the Scots' advance, but the Scottish pikemen drove them off and inflicted heavy casualties on the English horsemen. The Scottish army was by now stalled and under heavy attack on three sides from ships cannons, artillery, archers, and arquebusiers (soldiers with portable long-barrelled guns, fired by matchlock) to which they had no reply. When the Scots broke, the English cavalry rejoined the battle and therein began the slaughter.

The Scots retreated with many being struck down as they fled. The slaughter continued for five miles landward toward Edinburgh, the River Forth running red with their blood and southward to Dalkeith. In all, about 14,000 had been slain. The battle of Pinkie Cleugh was a devastating defeat for Scotland. It is now known as 'Black Saturday.'

Many Scots blamed traitors within their own ranks for their defeat, but in reality, a Renaissance army had defeated a Medieval army. This was the last of the formal pitched battles and the first of the modern battles in the British Isles, and before the eventual establishment of the Union of the Crowns in 1603.

Even though they had suffered a resounding defeat in battle, the Scottish government refused to accept the marriage of Mary, Queen of Scots, to Edward VI. The infant Queen Mary was smuggled out to France to be betrothed to the young Francis II. Lord Somerset occupied Scottish strongholds and large parts of the Lowlands and Borders but failed to capture Edinburgh and Leith, so the battle was won, but the war was lost.

Religious change was established through the Scottish Reformation when the Scots broke away from the Roman Catholic Church in 1560. Through the influence of John Calvin, the Calvinist predominantly Presbyterian Scots Kirk (Church of Scotland) was established.

Battle of Ancrum Moor–1545

In 1545, the English army under Sir Ralph Eure continued to pillage throughout the Borders as part of the Rough Wooing. This was the first part of the wooing when Henry VIII was still alive. Eure's many atrocities included the burning of Brumehous Tower with the family and servants inside.

On 27th February 1545, having plundered the town of Melrose and its abbey, the English army camped at Lilliard Edge on Ancrum Moor on their way to Jedburgh. The English army consisted of 3,000 German mercenaries, 1,500 English hired from Northumberland, and 800 Scottish assured men who had sworn allegiance to the English crown.

When they saw a small Scottish cavalry troop riding from Peniel Heugh Hill (the distinctive peak that is now crowned by the Waterloo Monument), the English army turned to pursue them. The English army was divided into two groups. The vanguard comprised around 2,000 soldiers under Layton and the second group, led by Eure, consisted of approximately 3,000 men. Both groups were built up with cavalry, spearmen in the centre, one wing of archers, and the other of hagbutters carrying portable long-barrelled guns.

What Eure did not know was that the Scots had amassed a force of around 2,500, including lancers and Border reivers, among whom were approximately 200 Turnbulls.

Layton's cavalry and foot soldiers dashed uphill, thinking that they were attacking only a few men. As they neared the top, the main Scottish army came over the brow of the hill out of the bright setting sun, surprising the English vanguard and pushing them back into Eure's group. At that point, the assured men ripped off the red crosses sewn to their tunics and joined in the counter-attack on the English troops. The English lines collapsed in complete disarray, and a rout ensued, with the English army fleeing through a hostile Scottish countryside back towards England. Both Layton and Eure were killed, along with 800 of their soldiers and around 1,000 English prisoners were taken.

This battle stopped the rough wooing for a period until the death of Henry VIII, when it became even more violent. Hertford, now Lord Protector, and through the Duke of Somerset, ruled on behalf of Edward VI, seeking to accomplish in Scotland what Henry had not been able to do.

According to local legend, the Borders Maid Lilliard was a heroine in the battle of Ancrum Moor. She is said to have come from the town of Maxton that was viciously attacked by Eure, killing the residents including her family. Seeing her lover killed in the Ancrum Moor battle, she rushed in, picked up his sword and attacked the enemy.

Raid of the Redeswire—1575

On 7th July 1575 Sir John Carmichael, Warden of the Scottish West March met Sir John Forster, English Warden of the Middle Marches, at Carter Bar for a truce. Wary of each other Carmichael brought a few pikemen and gunmen, and Forster came with a small army.

Rather than a truce, the encounter started with insults that soon turned into a battle. The more numerous English were winning until the arrival of Turnbull reinforcements from the Rule Valley along with others from Jedburgh, leading to a Scottish victory.

The English were routed. George Heron, his brother John Heron, and many other English nobles were killed. The English Warden John Forster was captured along with many of his troops. They were well treated and then released, to foster peace.

The story of the battle was made into the Borders ballad, 'Raid of the Redeswire.' Near the battle site at Carter Bar in the Cheviot Hills, a commemorative monument was erected with a plaque that reads:

> *On this ridge, 7th June 1575, was fought one of the last border raids, known as, The Raid of the Redeswire.*

Notwithstanding that it wasn't a raid and it didn't occur in the Redeswire, except in the ballad, this was the last major battle between the two kingdoms.

Walter Baster - CC SA 3 0

The Redeswire Stone at Carter Bar

The 1600's

Battle of Philiphaugh–1645

The Battle of Philiphaugh in September 1645, was part of the Wars of Three Kingdoms. These were the conflicts that took place in England, Ireland and Scotland between the years of 1639 and 1651. In the case of the Battle of Philiphaugh, it was not the usual English versus Scots conflict. It was a Scottish civil war battle fought on Scottish soil between the Royalists, supporters of the king, and Covenanters who supported the covenant of 1638 that pledged to protect the Presbyterian religion.

On the 12th of September, James Graham, the Marquis of Montrose, a Scottish nobleman, arrived at Philiphaugh near Selkirk. Here he camped in a secure position at the junction of the Ettrick and Yarrow rivers. The two rivers to the south and the hills of Ettrick Forest to the north protected his camp. Meanwhile, Sir David Leslie, Commander of Scottish Forces that had been fighting in England, marched back into Scotland.

Norman Turnbull

By the 12th September, unknown to Montrose, who was camped nearby between Selkirk and Galashiels, Leslie had around 6,000 men, and Montrose only had about 700, as many of his Highland and Irish troops had gone back home and his recruiting efforts in the predominately Presbyterian Borders had received a lukewarm response.

Next morning, Leslie advanced towards Philiphaugh and split his army into two groups. One group, led by Agnew Lochnaw, moved northwards through the gap between Linglie Hill and Peat Law and attacked Montrose's troops from the rear. Leslie commanded the second group that marched along the river valley and captured the hopelessly outnumbered royalists by surprise. Montrose's men stood little chance. The hastily dug trenches proved inadequate, and although Montrose led a sprinted cavalry charge against Leslie's horsemen and fought bravely, his troops were driven back with heavy losses.

The lucky ones, including Montrose, escaped over Minch Moor. The Irish troops and supporters that surrendered were either massacred on the battlefield or while in captivity at nearby Newark Castle.

The 1700's

Battle of Culloden–1746

On 16th April 1746, the last pitched battle in Britain was fought at Culloden. This decisive battle took place in the Highlands, not in the Borders, but it is included because of its effect on all of Scotland, including the Borders.

Charles Edward Stuart, known as Bonnie Prince Charlie (The Young Pretender) raised an army to return the British throne to his father,

James III/VIII (The Old Pretender) and heir of James II/VII who had been deposed because he was Roman Catholic.

Bonnie Prince Charlie's army and its supporters of King James were known as the Jacobites, from the Latin *Jacobus* of James. After initial victories, including the Battle of Prestonpans, the Jacobite Army was forced to retreat to the area of most significant support in the Highlands to raise funds and recruits. The Jacobites were supported financially by France, that also supplied troops in the form of Scots units, in service to the king of France, including the Royal Scots.

David Morier, 1746

The Battle of Culloden

The Jacobites were pursued and engaged near Inverness by the British Government army led by Prince William, Duke of Cumberland, the son of the English King George II. His forces were comprised mostly of Protestant soldiers from England but also contained a large number of Scots from the Highlands, Borders, and Ulster. This made Culloden not only a battle between England and Scotland but also a Scottish religious civil battle.

When the Jacobites were decisively defeated in battle, not only the combatants but many civilian Jacobite supporters were executed or imprisoned and their homes burned. The 1746 Act of Proscription was passed to destroy the power of the Scots' clans, by banning traditional Highland dress, possession of arms, even bagpipes, which were said to be an 'instrument of war.'

The Act of Proscription flamed the rebellious spirit of the Scots who first found ways to resist its suppression and, over time, to romanticise the Jacobite cause in art, literature, poetry, ballads, and television presentations such as *Outlander.*

Borders Clan Tartans

Armstrong (ancient)

Elliot (ancient)

Kerr (ancient)

Scott (ancient)

Turnbull (ancient)

Turnbull (modern)

Trails

The Borders

W. Turnbull - CC SA 3.0

The Scottish Borders region once stretched from Eyemouth in the northeast to Carlisle in the southwest. Today the council area known as the Borders covers the eastern portion of the area between Edinburgh and the English border.

The main towns in the Borders developed along the River Tweed flowing past Peebles in the west to the sea at Berwick. Today the largest of the Borders towns are Peebles, Galashiels, Melrose, Selkirk, Hawick, Jedburgh, Kelso, and Eyemouth. We have included Eyemouth instead of Berwick, because the latter is now part of

England, though it remains culturally Scottish.

Until the 15th century the major Borders towns would have included the royal burgh of Roxburgh, which had as much strategic importance as Edinburgh, Stirling, Perth and Berwick during the Wars of Scottish Independence. The town and castle were destroyed in 1460. Today, the name Roxburgh is given to a small village about two miles southwest of the historic site of Roxburgh Castle. Roxburghshire retains the official status as a registration county, which covers roughly the same area known as Teviotdale.

Peebles

On the A703—27 miles south of Edinburgh (take A701 to B7026 to A703) / On the A72—19 miles west of Galashiels. Postcode EH45 8BB, (55.6532658, -3.2008346)

Founded as a market town, Peebles sits at the confluence of the River Tweed and Eddleston Water. The name is generally thought to be derived from the Brythonic Celtic *pebyll* tents (a temporary settlement).

W. Turnbull - CC SA 3.0

Old Parish Church High Street Peebles

Peebles is surrounded by some of the highest hills in the Borders, including the famous Glensax Horseshoe and Cademuir Hill, rising from the banks of the River Tweed. On the ridge above Cademuir are the remains of two substantial Iron Age forts that were home to a community of a thousand or more people. Both forts were abandoned when the Romans reached the area around 80 AD.

The John Buchan trail from Peebles to the top of Cademuir Hill provides a pleasant walk and a magnificent panorama of the countryside, including the Glensax Horseshoe.

The town of Peebles was partially surrounded by strategically placed walls that included four gates where the major roads led into the town, Eastgate, Northgate, Bridgegate, and Ludgate on the west. There is an old market cross at the intersection of Northgate and Eastgate (High Street).

The oldest building in Peebles is the tower of St. Andrew's Church, founded in 1195. It was severely damaged by the soldiers of Henry VIII during the Rough Wooing. The old Cross Kirk, founded in 1261, is mostly in ruins but continues to play an important part in the local Common Riding festival known as the Beltane.

To the west of the town is Neidpath Castle that can be reached on foot through Hay Lodge Park; the route offering spectacular views of the castle.

Neidpath Castle

On the A2—1 mile west of Peebles centre, Postcode EH45 9J, (55.652088, -3.214694)

Neidpath Castle was built in the 13th century by Sir Simon Fraser as a tower house above the River Tweed, with commanding views of the surrounding countryside.

The Hay family who constructed the current castle in the 14th century acquired the barony of Neidpath along with the castle. It was visited by Mary, Queen of Scots, in 1563 and by James VI in 1587.

Neidpath was attacked by Cromwell in 1650 and is reputed to have held out longer than any other Borders stronghold. The entrance is marked, and parking is available. It is also easily accessible on foot through Hay Lodge Park on the southwest side of Peebles. The foot trail offers excellent views of the castle from the riverside.

Guide Map

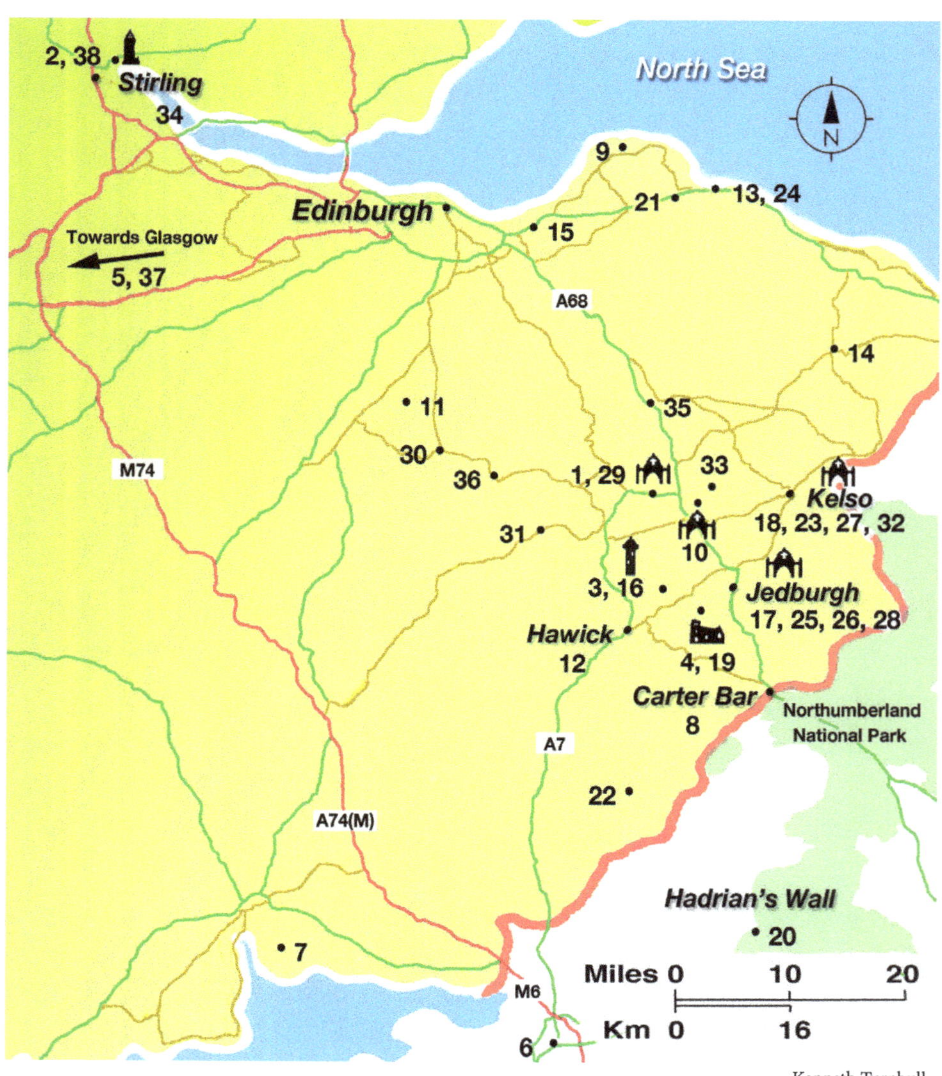

Kenneth Turnbull

1. Abbotsford House, **2**. Bannockburn Battle, **3**. Barnhills Castle, **4**. Bedrule Castle & Bedrule Kirk, **5**. Bothwell Castle, **6**. Carlisle Castle (England), **7**. Caerlaverock Castle, **8**. Carter Bar, **9**. Dirleton Castle, **10**. Dryburgh Abbey, **11**. Drochil Castle, **12**. Drumlanrig Tower, **13**. Dunbar Castle, **14**. Duns Castle, **15**. Fa'side Castle, **16**. Fatlips Castle, **17**. Ferniehirst Castle, **18**. Floors Castle, **19**. Fulton Tower, **20**. Hadrian's Wall, **21**. Hailes Castle, **22**. Hermitage Castle, **23**. Hume Castle, **24**. Innerwick Castle, **25**. Jedburgh Abbey, **26**. Jedburgh Castle, **27**. Kelso Abbey, **28**. Mary, Queen of Scots' House, **29**. Melrose Abbey, **30**. Neidpath Castle, **31**. Newark Castle, **32**. Roxburgh Castle, **33**.Smailholm Tower, **34**. Stirling Castle, **35**.Thirlestane Castle, **36**. Traquair House, **37**. University of Glasgow, **38**. Wallace Monument

Drochil Castle

Off the A72—8 miles west of Peebles. A72 8 miles to B7509. Postcode EH46 7DD, (55.677403, -3.332570)

Sitting above the Lyne Water, Drochil Castle was started by James Douglas, 4th Earl of Morton, Regent of Scotland, in 1578. Three years later, while the castle was still under construction, Douglas was accused by James Stuart of complicity in the murder of Henry Stuart, Lord Darnley, the father of the young King James VI. Even though he denied any participation, he was condemned for confessing knowledge of the plot and executed by the 'Maiden' an early form of guillotine. The partially completed castle was never finished. In 1686, it was purchased by William Douglas, 1st Duke of Queensberry, and the ruins are still owned by his descendant, the Duke of Buccleuch.

Paul Hermans - CC SA 3.0

Drochil Castle

Innerleithen

On the A72—7 miles east of Peebles / 12 miles west of Galashiels. Postcode EH44 6QR (55.618162, -3.065786)

The remains of an Iron Age hill fort on Caerlee Hill is evidence that Innerleithen was inhabited before Roman times.

The town name comes from the Scottish Gaelic for 'entrance of the Leithen,' as it sits at the confluence of the Leithen and the Tweed rivers. The prefix *Inner* or *Inver* is often used for Scottish place names of river confluence.

Dauntless111 - CC SA 3.0

Innerleithen

Innerleithen is said to have been founded by an itinerant pilgrim monk called St. Ronan in 737 AD. The Celtic stone known as the Runic Cross is located in the courtyard of the parish church on Leithen Road and was found nearby, suggesting that a church had existed here during the Early Middle Ages.

Traquair House

Off the A72—1.5 miles south of the A72 in Innerleithen south on Traquair Road. Follow signs for Traquair House from the A72 road as it passes through Innerleithen. Postcode EH44 6QZ, (55.608348, -3.063984)

Andy Stephenson - CC SA 2.0

Traquair House

Traquair House, 7 miles southeast of Peebles, is the oldest continually inhabited house in Scotland. Visited by 27 Scottish kings and queens, Traquair dates back to 1107, when it was built as a hunting lodge for Scottish kings. The Stuart family has lived there since 1491.

Bonnie Prince Charlie visited his distant cousin, the 5th Earl at Traquair, also named Charles Stuart, in 1745 on his march through the recently United Kingdom attempting to retake the throne for his father. As the prince departed through the Bear Gates, the earl ordered the gates at the top of the avenue to be shut after him, until the Stuarts returned to the throne. They have remained locked and known as the *Steekit Yetts* (stuck gates) since that time.

Galashiels

On the A7—33 miles south of Edinburgh / On the A6091—7 miles west of the A68 at the Ravenswood Roundabout. Postcode TD1 1EU, (55.613846, -2.808042)

Galashiels, often called just Gala, sits in the valley of the Gala Water River at its confluence with the River Tweed in the centre of the Scottish Borders. Its name is derived from the Gaelic *shiels* (dwellings) on the Gala River. The first recorded reference to the town is in an

1124 charter during the reign of David I, where it was referred to as *Galche.* Gala is mentioned in the writings of Blind Harry in 1296, when he refers to William Wallace's pursuit of Cospatrick, Earl of Dunbar, who had taken refuge on top of Gala Hill.

In 1321, Robert the Bruce granted Ettrick Forest and the royal hunting lodge, known as Hunters Hall to Sir James Douglas. The Earl of Douglas later granted the lairdship of Galashiels to the Pringle family.

Galashiels

At the Battle of Flodden, the Laird of Galashiels and four of his five sons were killed. His fifth son, who had been left behind, became the next laird. Eventually, the last direct descendant of the Pringle family was a female. When she married a Scott, that family became the lairds of Galashiels.

The Galashiels coat of arms shows two foxes reaching up to eat plums from a tree, with the motto, 'Sour Plums,' pronounced by the Scots as 'soor plooms.' It is a reference to an incident in 1337 during Edward III's invasion of Scotland. A raiding party of English soldiers were picking wild plums close to the town and were caught by the Scots who came across them by chance and slaughtered them all at a place opposite Abbotsford, known to this day as the 'Englishmen's Syke.' The villagers have dubbed themselves, 'the Sour Plums o' Galashiels.' as they had proved to be more sour than the fruit the invaders had been gathering.

Thirlestane Castle

Off the A68—1 mile east on the A697. A68 3/4 mile south of Lauder to A697 1/2 mile northeast to Thirlestane Castle. Postcode TD2 6RU, (55.722045, -2.742253)

Thirlestane Castle borders Lauder that has for centuries, been on the direct route between Northumberland and Edinburgh. Today, that historic route through the Lauderdale valley of the Leader Water is followed by the A68.

By the end of the first millennium, a large fort existed on Castle Hill above the Leader Water near where Thirlestane Castle now stands.

The Maitlands who built Thirlestane, arrived with William the Conqueror in 1066, and soon settled in Northumberland. They gained power and wealth in Scotland as a result of their military service and political connections and have been influential in Scottish history for the better part of 800 years. William Maitland of Lethington was Secretary to Mary, Queen of Scots. His younger brother, Sir John Maitland who was Chancellor to James VI of Scotland, acquired Thirlestane in 1587. He built a large Borders tower house on the foundations of the original fort.

When John Maitland was made the 1st Lord Maitland of Thirlestane in 1590, he moved the family residence to its current position. He built a large three storey stone keep with a circular drum tower at each corner.

Jo Turner - CC SA 2.0

Thirlestane Castle

Today, that original keep still lies at the core of the castle. Later, John's grandson, also John, was Charles II's Secretary of State for Scotland and more or less, governed the nation on the king's behalf. Using his position and wealth, he turned the castle into a palace.

One of the rooms in Thirlestane is known as Bonnie Prince Charlie's Room, as in 1745, following the Battle of Prestonpans, the Prince stayed there.

Melrose

On the A6091—5 miles east of the A7 at the Kingsknowe Roundabout / On the A6091—3 miles west of the A68 at the Ravenswood Roundabout. Postcode TD6 9LG, (55.599111, -2.718097)

Melrose from the Gaelic *Maolros*, (bald moor) or (bare peninsula) refers to the original site of the monastery in a bend of the river Tweed. This is one the most beautiful towns in all of Scotland.

When the town's monastery was expanded and relocated to its

present position by David I in the early 12th century, the name of the abbey and town were changed to play on the words 'mell' (mason's hammer) and 'rose' (symbol of the Virgin Mary) to whom the abbey was dedicated.

The town of Melrose is home to the famous Melrose Rugby Sevens, the oldest rugby sevens competition that dates from 1883, and attracts teams from around the world.

Melrose Abbey

Off the A6091 on Abbey Street in Melrose. Postcode TD6 9LG, (55.599111, -2.718097)

St. Mary's Abbey, Melrose (Melrose Abbey) was originally founded in 1136, as a monastery by Cistercian Monks. It was built in the Gothic form of St. John's cross at the request of King David I of Scotland who paid for its construction. It was one of four Borders abbeys, including Kelso, Jedburgh and Dryburgh. The town of Melrose grew up around the abbey and became one of the biggest wool producers in Britain.

Kenneth Turnbull

Melrose Abbey

The Cistercian Order of Monks based at the abbey, were very diligent hardworking men. Their life was dedicated to prayer and physical labour. They were known as the 'white monks,' because they wore garments of white woollen fabric Guided by the Abbot, they took care of the spiritual need of the inhabitants in the surrounding area.

There are eight aisle chapels that have survived at Melrose Abbey, including the last three to be constructed during the time that William Turnbull was Abbot of Melrose, between 1503-1506.

Abbot Turnbull's faint initials can still be seen on the back wall of the third chapel when looking to the west. Among the carved decorations on the buttresses that support the aisle chapels, the shield of Abbot William Turnbull and that of King James the IV (dated 1505) are displayed.

In 1333, the heart of King Robert the Bruce was buried in the Melrose Abbey in a silver casket. His body was interred in Dunfermline Abbey on his death in 1329. There are two legends about the heart. The first, that on his deathbed, Bruce had instructed that it be interred in Melrose Abbey. The second is that he instructed Sir James Douglas to carry it on a crusade to the Holy Land.

During the Wars of Scottish Independence, Melrose, like the other great abbeys, was in the forefront of the conflict. The army of King Edward II of England badly damaged it in 1322. King Robert the Bruce helped the Monks to rebuild the abbey, that lasted until the 16th-century Reformation, when it fell into ruin, though it continued to be used as a parish church until 1810. Today, it is often used as a romantic setting for weddings.

Abbotsford House

Off the A6091—3 miles west of Melrose—TD6 9BQ, (55.599541, -2.782084)

LeCardinal - CC SA 3.0

Abbotsford House

This Gothic baronial mansion was the magnificent country residence of the novelist and poet, Sir Walter Scott. Now open to the public, it is not only a museum, but operates as a functions venue and also offers luxury accommodations.

Carved crest versions of local Scottish clans decorate Abbotsford, including the name of Turnbull, which adorns one of the beam cornice supports in the library.

Eildon Hill

One mile South of Melrose about 3 hours there and back by foot. (55.587086, -2.708237)

The name is usually pluralised into The Eildons or Eildon Hills, because of its triple peak. The 1,385-foot northeast hilltop (Eildon North) is surrounded by over three miles of ramparts enclosing around forty acres into which over 300 terraces have been cut into the hillside to provide bases for turf houses.

Kenneth Turnbull

The three peaks of Eildon Hill seen from Scott's View

The Eildon Hills are often snow covered in winter. Forests containing deer, badgers, stoats, and foxes surround them. A monument to Sir Walter Scott sits atop the highest hilltop.

There is substantial archaeological evidence that that the hill was occupied in the Bronze age before 1000 BC as a fort. At its peak, the population of the hill fort may have been more than 5,000; the most significant known settlement in Scotland at that time.

The Romans built their vast Fort Trimontium, named for the three peaks at the foot of the hill on the bank of the River Tweed, in the first century. At the same time, they constructed a signal tower on the summit of the hill.

Scott's View

On the B6356—3 miles east of Melrose and 3 miles north of St. Boswells. A68 to B6404 in St. Boswells east ~2 miles to B6356 north ~3 miles. Postcode TD6 9, (55.600269, -2.646804)

Looking out over the valley of the River Tweed, the view from this vantage point is reputed to be the favourite of Sir Walter Scott for whom it is named.

It is said that Scott stopped for the view so often, that his horse began stopping on the spot without command. There is an expansive view to the west over a bend in the River Tweed to the three peaks of the Eildon Hills. The view looking to the southwest overlooks the village of Newtown St. Boswells and the surrounding countryside. Sunset from Scott's View is indeed a memorable experience.

Trimonteum Museum

In the Ormiston building on Melrose Market Square next to the Burt's Hotel Postcode. TD6 9PN (55.5970348, -2.7201731)

The Trimontium Museum (Three Hills Roman Heritage Centre) tells the story of a Roman Frontier Post and its first-century occupants. This is a small but unique museum and well worth a visit.

The museum contains artefacts, replicated displays, and information about both the first and second Roman military complexes built at Trimontium. There is also a fascinating video available on Hadrian's Wall and the Antonine Wall.

During the summer months, guided walks leave from the museum at 13:30 on Tuesdays and Thursdays returning by 17:30.

Dryburgh Abbey

On the B6356—4 miles east of the A68. A68 to B6404 east through St. Boswells to B6356 north then west. (The abbey is less than a mile from the A68, but access over the Tweed River requires a longer drive. Alternately, there is a mile long footpath to the abbey from the car park on High Street in St. Boswells.) Postcode TD6 6RQ, (55.577092, -2.6497)

Dryburgh, which is considered by many to be the most beautiful of all the Borders Abbeys, is also special because its ruins are remarkably complete. The Dryburgh chapter house is especially well preserved, allowing the visitor to imagine a monk's life in the 12th century.

It is believed that the loop in the River Tweed, now occupied by

Dryburgh Abbey was settled in the 6th century by St. Modan, the son of an Irish chief and early Christian missionary to Scotland.

The Dryburgh Abbey, which dates back to 1150, was burned down three times but remains an example of some of the best Gothic church architecture in Scotland. Its transepts are exceptionally beautiful. One can admire the cloister and chapter house, that contains fragments of painted wall plaster dating from early construction. Dryburgh Abbey is the burial place of Sir Walter Scott.

Kenneth Turnbull

Dryburgh Abbey

As a Borders Abbey, Dryburgh suffered multiple English attacks through the centuries. It is said that in 1322, while retreating south to England following their unsuccessful attack on Edinburgh, Edward II's army took exception to the sound of Dryburgh Abbey's bells being rung to celebrate their defeat. In frustrated revenge, they burned the abbey, as well as the one at Melrose.

Selkirk

On the A7—40 miles south of Edinburgh—7 miles south of Galashiels. Postcode TD7 4AA , (42.815804, -79.957876)

Walter Baxter - CC SA 2.0

Selkirk

Selkirk is one of the oldest royal burgh settlements in the Scottish Borders. The name 'Selkirk' (church in the forest) derives from the Old English *sele* (hall) and *cirice* (church). It was the site of the first Borders abbey in 1113.

The first church was that of the local Selgovae tribe who converted to Christianity in the 6th century. It was in the church at Selkirk that William Wallace was declared Guardian of the Kingdom of Scotland. This is also the gravesite of a number of relatives of Franklin D. Roosevelt, the 32nd president of the USA.

Selkirk men fought with Wallace at Stirling Bridge and Falkirk and with Robert the Bruce at Bannockburn. But it is the Battle of Flodden in 1513 for which Selkirk warriors are most remembered. Only the one man, known as Fletcher, returned from Flodden, carrying a bloodstained English flag that he had captured from the Macclesfield regiment. As he reached Selkirk, Fletcher wrapped the captured English standard around his head and fell to his death. The English subsequently sacked and burned the town.

Sir Walter Scott was appointed Sheriff-Deputy of Selkirk County in 1799 and dispensed justice for 33 years to the people of Selkirkshire from the town square courthouse.

Marc Turú

Selkirk Auld Kirk

The oldest surviving and one of the most picturesque narrow walkways is Halliwell's Close. Over the past 400 years, many tradesmen lived and worked along this lane, including weavers, fleshers (butchers) ironmongers, tailors, bakers, coopers (barrel makers) and shoemakers. A former home and ironmonger's shop, now the Halliwell's House Museum, recreates the building's former use. It tells the story of the atmospheric close, the history of Selkirk, and the town's common riding.

Philiphaugh Battle Site

Junction of A707 and A708 on the west side of Selkirk now show Selkirk rugby and cricket pitches. Postcode TD7 5AU, (55.546415, -2.859020)

Walter Baxter - CC SA 2.0

Philiphaugh Cairn

An information panel and memorial cairn are located on the Philiphaugh Estate, 1 mile west of Selkirk on the A708. The information panel can be found in the car park, signposted as Salmon Viewing Centre on the south side of the A708.

The cairn monument site is not signposted. It is 3/4 of a mile west of the Salmon Viewing Centre on the opposite side of the A708, in the trees.

Newark Castle

Off the A708—5 miles west of Selkirk. A708 west 3 miles to A707 2 miles. Postcode TD7 5EU, (55.554770, -2.919767)

Archibald Douglas, Earl of Wigtown, began the construction of Newark Castle in 1423, on a rocky knoll overlooking the River Yarrow. Its name, New Wark (New Castle) replaced Auld Wark that stood to the east. The old site has been lost to the construction and landscaping of Bowhill House. Newark Castle grew to become a large tower house of five storeys, possessing a garret, a corbelled parapet and caphouses, with a gatehouse and rectangular towers that flank it. As well, it contains an unusually high number of gunloops and stands in the centre of a barmkin (outer fortification) now in ruins, which likely encased the whole summit of the knoll.

Newark Castle was seized by King James III, following his overthrow of the Douglases in 1455. In 1473, the king gifted Newark Castle to his queen, Margaret of Denmark. The royal arms are visible on the west gable of the tower. The castle was besieged unsuccessfully by the English army in 1547 but was taken and burned in 1548. In 1645, following the Battle of Philiphaugh, around 100 royalist followers of the Marquis of Montrose, including women and children, were shot in the barmkin. The castle is believed to be haunted by those poor souls who can be heard on 13th September of each year. The mass grave of those murdered was located nearby in 1810, in a field known as Slain Men's Lea.

Newark Castle

The Newark Castle Tower House is now part of the grounds of Bowhill House.

Hawick

On the A7—51 miles south of Edinburgh—18 miles south of Galashiels. / On the A698—11 miles west of Jedburgh. Postcode TD9 9EF, (55.427060, -2.780914)

The town's name is derived from 'haw' (hawthorn bush) and the Middle English word 'wik' (village). Possibly because the original settlement was surrounded by a hawthorn hedge for protection.

Hawick provides an excellent base for those who visit the Borders with the purpose of exploring the many historical sites. It is not only convenient for exploration around the Scottish border sites but those on the other side of the nearby English border as well.

The town itself is steeped in history from facts to myths, from the old fortifications, burial grounds, kirkyards, towers, and tweed mills from the more recent past.

Drumlanrig Tower

At the west end of Hawick High Street—near the junction of the A698 and A7.
1 Tower Knowe, Hawick. Postcode TD9 9BZ, (55.4217141, -2.7912066)

Drumlanrig Tower, known today as the Borders Textile Towerhouse, is Hawick's oldest building. It was constructed as a 16th-century tower house by the Douglases of Drumlanrig and served as one of the town's primary defences.

When Thomas Howard, the Earl of Surrey, marched through the Borders in 1570, the citizens of Hawick burned the town to make it uninhabitable by the invaders. The only building that remained standing was the charred Drumlanrig Tower that became known as the Black Tower.

W. Turnbull - CC SA 3.0

Turnbull Clan flag at the Hawick Town Hall

In 1769, Drumlanrig Tower Castle was renovated into a popular inn for travellers going back and forth between Edinburgh and Carlisle. It remained a hotel for over 200 years until 1985, when the Roxburgh District Council purchased it.

Now, owned by the Scottish Borders Council, Drumlanrig Tower has been beautifully restored as a museum with period rooms, figures, and audiovisuals, that explain the turbulent past of the town and the tower. Information on the local knitwear industry and woollen mills has also been included.

The Hawick Tourist Information Centre is located in Drumlanrig Tower.

Turning of the Bull Monument

At the Hawick Heritage Hub—southern end of High Street near the junction of the Slitrig Water and the Teviot River. Postcode TD9 0AE, (55.4209074, -2.7956265)

W. Turnbull - CC SA 3.0

***Turning of the Bull* Monument at the Hawick Heritage Hub**

The *Turning of The Bull* Monument is a striking bronze statue, sculpted by Borders artist Angela Hunter. It depicts William Rule (Will-o'-Roul) turning a wild bull to save the life of King Robert the Bruce. The monument, erected by the Turnbull Clan Association in 2009, is unusual in its design, as it commemorates an act of bravery in saving a life.

Hawick Heritage Hub

Located in the heart of Hawick and next to the *Turning of the Bull* Monument, is the Heritage Hub, where visitors have the opportunity of tracing their family history.

This can be done on site through the availability of many categories of material, as well as from archived records from as far back as 1610. Online research is also available at heartofhawick.co.uk.
The Heritage Hub includes census records together with many Electoral Registers and Owners and Occupiers of Land documents. The Hub also holds a significant collection of copies of Valuation Rolls and Directories for the four Borders counties. However, original legal documents are only available in Edinburgh.

An extensive collection of maps dating back to 1791 is available. Local book publications, postcards and photographs can also be viewed. This is by no means an exhaustive listing of what is available.

Hornshole Battle

Off the A698—2 miles east of Hawick at the Hornshole Bridge, a few yards north of the A698. Postcode TD9 8SU, (55.442785, -2.739330)

Hornshole is commemorated by monuments at both ends of Hawick centre. In 1914 the now famous Horse Statue was erected at the northeast end of High Street. In 2014 a Quincentenary Statue of several figures, including one young callant raising a captured English flag, was placed outside Drumlanrig Tower.

Much of Hornshole's history is maintained in the culture of Hawick today, for example, the annual ride out that is celebrated, every summer and known as the Common Ridings. This old tradition of riding the boundaries of the town's territory is a very popular event.

Betty Turnbull - CC SA 3.0

Horneshole Quincentenary Statue

Teribus ye teri odin
Sons of heroes slain at Flodden
Imitating Border bowmen
Aye defend your rights and common

Hawick Motte

In Moat Park off the A7—near the junction of the A7 and the A698. 33D Loan, Hawick. Postcode TD9 0AX, (55.419657, -2.7931739)

Hawick Motte is a 12th-century earthwork flat-topped motte, founded by the Lovel family on land granted to the Norman lord by King David. The fortress stood on high ground above the west bank of Siltrig Water.

In 1912, an exploratory trench was cut across the filled in bailey, and it showed that the original trench had been between 5½ and 9½ yards wide, and between 1 and 2 ½ yards deep.

A coin of King Henry II, found in an excavation indicates a possible construction date of mid-1100's. The exact position of the bailey, that possibly lies uphill from the conical mound, has been lost. All that now remains are the remnants of the main earthen mound on which stood the defended buildings.

Hermitage Castle

On the B6399—16 miles south of Hawick. Postcode TD9 0LU, (55.2560337, -2.793231)

Kenneth Turnbull

Hermitage Castle

Known as the 'guardhouse of the bloodiest valley in Britain,' Hermitage Castle has been owned by some of the most important families in Scotland's history including the de Soulis, de Neville, Douglas, Hepburn, Stuart, and Scott families.

Hermitage was built by Nicholas de Soulis around 1240, as a typical Norman Motte and Bailey fort and subsequently improved through the centuries. The castle has a reputation, both from its history and its appearance, as one of the most sinister haunted castles in Scotland.

Mary, Queen of Scots, made a famous marathon journey on horseback from Jedburgh to visit her wounded lover James Hepburn, 4th Earl of Bothwell, at Hermitage. The 25-mile journey, which would have taken at least four hours each way, occurred only a few weeks after the birth of her son James VI/I in 1566. Mary and Bothwell were to marry in May 1567, shortly after the February murder of her 2nd husband, Henry Stuart (known as Lord Darnley) despite the fact that Bothwell was implicated in the murder.

Langholm

On the A7—23 miles southwest of Hawick. Postcode DG13 0DH, (55.1517378, -3.0170657)

Robert Matthews - CC SA 3.0

Known locally as the 'Muckle Toun,' Langholm is the home of the Armstrong clan and the birthplace of Thomas Telford the famous engineer and architect. Recognised as an important central town of the Border reivers, Langholm is surrounded by four hills and located by the River Esk.

Langholm has scenic and historical attractions including the Armstrong clan's Langholm Castle and the nearby site of the 1455 Arkinholm battle; a Scottish family feud between the Clan Douglas and the Stewart royal family.

Denholm

On the A698—5 miles east of Hawick. Postcode TD9 8PG, (55.4586043, -2.7001177)

The River Rule, which runs through Bonchester and Bedrule joins the River Teviot just south of Denholm village.

There is a story that during a Sunday service in earlier times, two boys from the village of Denholm unearthed a skeleton in the graveyard, and on selecting two large leg bones, concealed them on their person. They then took the bones home to Denholm. It was thought that the bones were those of Will-o'-Rule Turnbull as they were very long, indicating that they had come from an unusualy tall person. When the parents of the two boys discovered what the lads had done, they took the bones and buried them somewhere in the village to avoid retribution. To this day, they remain undiscovered.

Renata - CC SA 3.0

John Leyden Monument (his house in background)

There is a monument next to the A698 on the Denholm green to Dr John Leyden who was born in Denholm in 1775 and authored the epic poem *Scenes of Infancy: Descriptive of Teviotdale*. His father, a shepherd, sent John to Edinburgh University to study for the ministry. He completed his studies but realised that this was not his vocation. After graduation, he met Sir Walter Scott, who was at the time, collecting materials for his *Minstrelsy of the Scottish Borders*. As a Borderer himself, John soon became involved in border ballads and folklore. He edited the 16th-century edition of *The Complaynt of Scotland* and added an essay on Scottish folk music and customs.

Over time, Dr John Leyden managed to vary his vocations, including an appointment in India on the medical staff, then as a naturalist, a judge, and a court commissioner. Manuscripts found in the British library, indicate he also translated some Punjab works into English. In 1811, he joined an expedition to Java, where he, unfortunately, contracted malaria or dengue fever and died.

Rulewater

The Rulewater begins as many tiny streams flowing out of the Wauchope Forest on the north slopes of the Cheviot Hills along the border with England. It becomes a modest river, which joins the Teviot just south of Denholm village. The valley through which the Rulewater flows is the ancestral home of the Turnbull clan. That valley once boasted a much larger population than it has today. Its numerous towns have either dwindled to villages and hamlets or disappeared entirely.

Bedrule

Off the A698—5 miles west of Jedburgh, 1 mile south of the A698 / Off the A698—2 miles east of Denholm, 1 mile south of the A698 (There is a small signpost for Bedrule on the A698 about 5 miles west of Jedburgh. The road to Bedrule goes south from the A698 for a little more than a mile). Postcode TD9 8TE, (55.453677, -2.634779)

Bedrule was home to the Clan Comyn (Cumming), who had come from the town of Comines in northern France at the time of the Norman invasion, until John III (Red) Comyn was killed by Robert the Bruce. There is a 14th-century charter by Robert I granting Bedrule, called Bethocrule, to James Douglas who, in turn, granted it to the Turnbulls for protection against the English.

Bishop William Turnbull, who founded Glasgow University, was born in Bedrule around 1400.

W. Turnbull - CC SA 3.0

Bedrule Kirk and Rubers Law

The Bedrule kirkyard provides a spectacular view of Rubers Law rising to the west above the Rule Valley.

The kirk contains beautiful stained glass windows and a number of plaques about the Turnbulls and other families.

Kenneth Turnbull

Bedrule Kirk is a listed building of regional and high local importance. Sunday worship services are conducted on a regular basis.

There is a cairn conceived by Norman Turnbull in the kirkyard with a descriptive plaque commemorating the important influence of Bedrule Castle in the history of the Borders and the Turnbull reivers.

Fittingly, Bedrule kirkyard is usually a quiet place with only the sounds of the wind, birds, and the rumble of the Rulewater in the nearby valley below the church.

Bedrule Castle

Follow directions to Bedrule. The castle mound is 100 yards north of the kirk. Postcode TD9 8TE, (55.454662, -2.636694)

Prior to the building of the stone Bedrule Castle in the 1200s, another castle had stood on a mound some 350 yards to the west in a bend in the Rule River. That mound and its first fort are thought to have been built during the Iron Age and expanded, possibly with a moat at some stage in the Middle Ages during which time it was known as Fast Castle.

The Castle at Bedrule was a well-fortified dwelling for the Turnbull Clan. It was the largest and oldest oval shaped stronghold that stood high at the head of the Rule Valley. Two miles to the north of Bedrule Castle, beyond the Teviot River can be seen Fatlips Castle, another part of the Turnbull Teviotdale stronghold.

One of the most powerful names in Scotland's history was the Clan Comyn who built Bedrule Castle in the 1200's. The Comyn family also entertained callers to the castle. One of the distinguished guests was King Edward I during his Scottish visit in 1298.

When Robert the Bruce murdered John (Red) Comyn in Dumfries on the 10th February 1306, this improved his political ambitions to such an extent that within weeks, he was crowned King of Scotland at Scone. The death of Red Comyn saw their lands progressively forfeited. King Robert gave Bedrule to Sir James Douglas (The Black

Douglas) as the English called him, for safekeeping. The Turnbulls demonstrated themselves loyal to Douglas who was an important supporter of the king.

In time, the Turnbulls became a renowned Borders reiver clan, seated not just at Bedrule Castle, but also at Fatlips Castle on the top of the Minto Crags and Barnhill at the bottom of the same crags.

Igor Adasikov - Taimy Studios

Painting of Bedrule Castle, based on a 1984 survey of the castle ruins, with Turnbull 'Fatlips' Castle in the background atop Minto Crags

Bedrule became the principal seat of the Turnbulls and remained in their heritable possession until nearly the end of the 18th century. The English destroyed Bedrule Castle, among other Scottish Borders strongholds in 1545, during their devastating 'Rough Wooing' raids.

During the Rough Wooing raids meant to force Scotland to agree to a marriage alliance between its child Queen Mary and Edward, the heir apparent son of King Henry VIII, twelve castles, including Bedrule, were plundered and burned. As they were deadly enemies of the English, wherever a raid took place in the Middle Marches, the Turnbulls were invariably involved.

Today the remains of Bedrule castle, located 100 yards to the north of the church, consist of large grass-covered mounds and a few ground level foundation walls above the steep bank of the Rule Water. A drystone dyke cuts across the site where the remaining front section has been cleared, adding to the arable land of the adjoining field.

Rubers Law

About 1.5 miles southeast of Denholm and 1.5 miles southwest of Bedrule. (55.443845, -2.660454)

As one drives southwest from Bedrule towards Abbotrule and Bonchester Bridge, Rubers Law (mountain) rises to the north on the far side of the Rulewater river, which runs roughly parallel to the road. Rubers Law stands between the Rule and Teviot rivers.

Sunny Bedrule Photography

Rubsers Law

Several forts have been built on the summit of Rubers Law through the ages. The earliest was an *oppidum* (Iron Age hill fort). The remains of the outer wall of that fort can still be seen encircling an area of around 7 acres, with a visible entrance to the south.

The presence of Roman period dressed sandstone blocks on the hill, many with a diamond pattern on them, indicates that there was once a Roman signal station and fort. The same type of stones and decoration have been found at Castlecary on the Antonine Wall, confirming a Rubers Law Roman construction.

In 1863, a farmer, while digging field drains 400 feet from the top on the south-east side of the hill, discovered remnants of Roman bronze vessels, including a decorated handle of an ewer (large wide mouth jug) and fragments of many other vessels. These are now in the Hawick Museum.

A Middle Age nuclear fort was built on Rubers Law from loose boulders and the remains of the Roman fort. That fort enclosed a number of hut dwellings for protection of the residents.

During the latter part of the 17th-century, Covenanters commonly gathered on Rubers Law to worship. The location isolated them from the law and provided a good lookout position. From the name 'Peden's Pulpit,' given to a chasm in the cliff near the top, it appears probable that Alexander Peden preached to a conventicle of Covenanters there at least once.

The restoration of King Charles II as King of England, Scotland and Ireland in 1660, was followed by his attempt to impose Episcopal worship on the Church of Scotland. The Covenanters were those pledged to maintain the Kirk's Presbyterian worship. Alexander Peden and other ministers who left or were ejected from the Kirk preached to illegal conventicles of open-air worshipers between 1660 and 1688.

On Easter Day in 2000, an open-air service was held at the top of Rubers Law. Worshipers from the Rule Valley including Bedrule, Denholm, and Minto, gathered to commemorate the two thousandth anniversary of the birth of Jesus Christ and the sacrifice of earlier Christians who had worshipped there. That event is recorded on a metal plate fixed to a rock at the summit. Bedrule church now holds a service of worship on Rubers Law each Easter Day.

John Leyden described his walk up to Rubers Law in his poem *Scenes of Infancy*.

Oft have I wandered, in my vernal years,
Where Ruberslaw his misty summit rears,
And, as the fleecy surges closed amain,
To gain the top have traced that shelving lane,
Where every shallow stripe of level green,
That, winding, runs the shattered crags between

In another passage, he described a storm on the hill, and the presence of eagles that were known as 'erne.'

Dark Rubers Law, that lifts his head sublime,
Rugged and hoary with the wrecks of time!
On his broad misty front the giant wears
The horrid furrows of ten thousand years;
His aged brows are crowned with curling fern,
Where perches, grave and lone, the hooded Erne,
Majestic bird! by ancient shepherds stiled
The lonely hermit of the russet wild,
That loves amid the stormy blast to soar,
When through disjointed cliffs the tempests roar,
Climbs on strong wing the storm, and, screaming high,
Rides the dim rack, that sweeps the darkened sky.

—*Scenes of Infancy*, John Leyden

Fulton Tower

On Chesters Road—1.6 miles south of Bedrule. Postcode TD9 8TF, (55.434580, -2.625)

Fulton Tower near Bedrule

Built as a stronghold for the Fulton family in the 1400s, the tower was one of those destroyed by the Earl of Hertford during his 1545 Rough Wooing raids.

In 1566, Mary, Queen of Scots, stopped by the rebuilt Fulton Tower on her remarkable horseback journey from Jedburgh to visit her wounded lover James Hepburn at Hermitage Castle.

The towerhouse and lands passed to William Turnbull of Bedrule by marriage in 1570.

There is a Borders legend that the last person who inhabited Fulton Tower was a Turnbull engaged in a deadly feud with the Kerrs of Ferniehirst. The story has it that the Kerrs got access to the tower by stealth and surprised Turnbull who was holding his infant child on his knee. While the gudewife prepared the sowans for supper he was amusing their child by singing the old 'Highland Muster Roll.'

Little wat ye wha's comin',
Little wat ye wha's comin',
Jock and Tam and a's comin'!

The Kerrs rushed in exclaiming, 'Little wat ye wha's coming indeed.' Though totally unprepared, Turnbull managed to jump up, seize his sword, and being a powerful man, was preparing to fight. The tearful pleading of his wife begging him not to risk the life of their baby caused him to surrender. What became of him, after he had thus fallen into the hands of his enemies, the writer has not been able to learn.[4]

Abbotrule

Off the B6357—9 miles south of Bedrule, 1 mile southwest of the B6357, and 1/2 mile southwest of Jedforest Hunt farm. Postcode TD9 8JD, (55.405774, -2.616661)

Most of the villages along the Rulewater have only a few stone walls remaining to mark what was once a bustling centre of activity.

In a field overlooking a modern working farm, are the remains of a very old kirk and gravestones. All that remains are the two gable ends of the kirk. In its day, that Abbotrule kirk was the worship place for many of the prominent Turnbulls who lived along the Rulewater.

---

4 *The Statistical Account of Roxburghshire by the Ministers of the Respective Parishes*, William Blackwood and Sons, Edinburgh, Scotland, 1841, p. 284.

Abbotrule Kirk demolished by Patrick Kerr in 1774

It seems that when Abbotrule came under the influence of Patrick Kerr, the kirk and kirkyard were in the way of one who had no love for the kirk and who could not tolerate ministers. The kirk and kirkyard of Abbotrule, which can still be seen, lay near the Laird's house. This intolerable situation resulted in drastic action by the Laird of Abbotrule, who decided to rid himself of his neighbours.

For years Patrick Kerr had bided his time and a well-pleased man was he, when in 1744, he had Elliot of Stobes and Douglas of Douglas to side with him. He wiped out forevermore the Abbotrule kirk and parish enabling him to seize its lands.

With the Abbotrule kirk demolished, in 1777 Abbotrule parish was annexed to the parishes of Hobkirk and Southdean.

The Abbotrule parish twenty-five-acre glebe (portion) of good land should have been shared between the Southdean and Hobkirk parishes, but Patrick Kerr kept it for his own use. Instead, fifty acres of poor soil lying between Doorpool and Chesters was given to the parishes. He must have had pleasure in this bargain, for he had gained a fertile glebe and had forever freed himself from his priestly neighbours. Wasting no time, he sought to plough up the kirkyard, but this could not be done because it was considered sacred ground. Burials continued there for 100 years after Patrick Kerr was gone.

Southdean

Nearby Southdean is yet another small hamlet by the Rule Water in the Wauchope Forest area. It is here where the remains of Dykeraw Tower and Southdean Old Parish Kirk can still be found.

Bonchester Bridge

On the A6088—6 miles southeast of the A698. Postcode TD9 8JN, (55.400175, -2.655392)

The village of Bonchester Bridge is located on the Rule Water between Abbotrule and Hobkirk. On the edge of the village can be seen the remains of medieval earthworks known as Duncan's Hole. To the east of Bonchester Bridge, Bonchester Hill rises to a height of 1059 ft and is topped by the ancient Roman fort called *Bonna Castra* (good camp).

Hobkirk

On the B6357—9 miles southwest of Jedburgh (A68 2 miles to B6357 7 miles). Postcode TD9 8JU, (55.387078, -2.654213)

Hobkirk village, also known as Hopekirk, is now a civil parish.

Part of the Abbotrule parish was annexed to Hobkirk in 1777. The present parish church was built in 1869.

The kirkyard has graves that date well back over the centuries, including famous Borders clan names such as Douglas, Scott, Elliot, Kerr, Graham, Turnbull, and others.

Hobkirk Kirk

As an additional interest, the visitor may like to take a small detour to the little village of Cavers. This was an area passed on by King Robert the Bruce to James Douglas, who was his trusted Lieutenant in the Battle of Bannockburn.

Jedburgh

On the A68—48 miles south of Edinburgh / On the A698 - 11 miles east of Hawick. Postcode TD8 6EN, (55.4778286, -2.5699647)

The frontier town of Jedburgh located on the Jed Water River is only 10 miles from the border with England at Carter Bar. The ruins of Jedburgh Abbey and the Jedburgh Castle Jail are at the west end of town, and the famous Mary, Queen of Scots House is in the centre of town.

Kenneth Turnbull

Jedburgh Abbey and kirkyard

Before Jedburgh became a burgh (a place of special privileges granted by King David I), it was previously known as Jedworth. There is a record of a 9th-century church in Jedburgh that King David I made into a monastery for Augustinian monks from France in the 12th century. English invasions in the 16th century left the monastery in ruin, though significant portions still remain.

King David also built a castle at Jedburgh as a royal residence. After his death, that castle was among those ceded to England in 1174. The castle was retaken by the Scots and demolished in 1409, being the last English stronghold in Scotland at that time. In 1823, a modern jail was built on the site of the castle. It was in 1964 when the jail was converted to the Jedburgh Castle Jail and Museum.

Jedburgh's proximity to England brought not only conflict but, during times of peace, wealth through trade, which extended not only to England, but also to the continent.

For many years Jedburgh was the county town of Roxburghshire and home of the Sheriff Court. As such, many from the Borders were tried and imprisoned or executed here for petty and capital crimes by the notorious sheriffs of Jedburgh.

The Old Jedburgh Jail (now a museum) is another historic attraction and well worth a visit. The Mary, Queen of Scots House is another recommended visit.

Jedburgh Abbey

In Jedburgh on the southwest side of town. Postcode TD8 6JQ, (55.476606, -2.554923)

In 1138, Jedburgh Abbey was founded, initially as a priory status, then in 1147, it became a fully-fledged Abbey, dedicated to the Virgin Mary.

Kenneth Turnbull

Jedburgh Abbey interior

In 1285, Alexander III married his second queen, Yolande de Dreux, in the Jedburgh Abbey. The church was magnificently decorated and thronged with guests when legend tells us; a ghostly figure appeared before the congregation and foretold the king's death. As it turned out, Alexander died in the following year. It was that death, followed by the sad death in 1290, of his infant granddaughter and heir, Margaret the Maid of Norway and the short, ill reign of John Balliol (1292-1296) that formed the prelude to the long and bloody Wars of Scottish Independence.

When King David I of Scotland died, the patronage and privileges of the abbey were accorded to his grandsons, Malcolm IV of Scotland and William I of Scotland. In 1297, the Abbey was pillaged and wrecked by the English as retribution for their earlier and humiliating defeat at the hands of William Wallace. Despite this, the church continued to be royally patronised.

The end came when the Abbey of St. Mary of Jedburgh was attacked and set on fire in 1523, with the town of Jedburgh also suffering heavy destruction at the hands of the English Earl of Hertford. By 1560, the great Abbey was transformed through the Scottish Reformation. However, the monks were allowed to stay. By 1871, the former Abbey was declared unsafe, and it is now in the care of Historic Scotland.

Jedburgh Castle, Jail, and Museum

In Jedburgh on the southwest side of town. Postcode TD8 6AS, (55.4742688, -2.564342)

Mihael Grmek - CC SA 3.0

Jedburgh Castle, Jail, and Museum

Jedburgh Castle was a dominant Scottish Borders defence guarding the old Roman route from Northumberland to Edinburgh. It was a frontier outpost, so the castle was continuously fought over during the Wars of Scottish Independence. The Castle was demolished in 1409, and a jail was constructed on the site in 1823. In 1847, the Jail's internal structure was altered to come into line with the Prison Acts of 1839 that amongst other things, specified separate cells. The jail is said to be the finest remaining Howard Reform prison in Scotland. Through the years, many Turnbulls have been temporary residents.

Today, the Jedburgh Castle Jail and Museum provides a fascinating history of the royal burgh of Jedburgh that gives visitors a feel for life in a 1820s prison, with an excellent view over the town.

Mary Queen Of Scots House

Queen St, Jedburgh. Postcode TD8 6EN, (55.478666, -2.5527102)

In 1566, Mary was in Jedburgh and heard that her lover, James Hepburn, the Earl of Bothwell, lay wounded at Hermitage Castle some 20 miles away. The headstrong queen rode by horseback to Hermitage and back to Jedburgh in one day. Bad weather made the journey worse. The queen's party got lost, and she fell into a bog on the way back. She arrived in Jedburgh close to death and spent time recuperating there.

Kenneth Turnbull

The Jedburgh death mask of Mary, Queen of Scots

The house where she sojourned belonged to the Kerrs of nearby Ferniehirst Castle. Because most of that clan was left-handed the unusual spiral staircase was built counterclockwise, enabling them to wield their sword more easily.

The house museum has memorabilia of Mary including jewellery, documents, paintings, and the watch Mary lost when she fell in the bog and was found 250 years later.

The Capon 'Hanging' Tree

On the A68—2 miles south of Jedburgh, on the bank of the Jed River, a few yards to the west of the road. (55.461113, -2.553969)

The Capon Tree is one of the few remaining original trees of the Jed Forest. Possibly as much as 1,000 years old, the hollow oak has a huge ten-foot diameter trunk, now split in two. The tree, designated as one of the 50 most significant trees in the United Kingdom, gets its name from the Capuchin monks of Jedburgh Abbey who were known to rest under it.

Kenneth Turnbull

The 1,000-year-old Capon Oak 'Hanging Tree'

The Capon Tree, a popular meeting place for border clans during the Middle Ages, became known as 'The Hanging Tree.' Today, the Capon Tree is the scene of one of the ceremonies held during The Callant's Festival. The Charter of 1502 named the festival after Jethart Callant, founder of the Borders Games Festival.

The festival is held in early July of each year, where the Callant and his cavalcade proceed to the Capon Tree where a sprig from it is pinned to the Callant's lapel by the president of the festival.

The Turnbulls were notorious reivers who ignored the laws of the king. They were indeed a rowdy group that had little or no respect for the laws meant to keep the lower class down. Reiving was not only a way of life but also another way to thumb their noses at the authorities that tried to control the clan.

In 1510, the Turnbulls had built a reputation for unruliness. Their disrespect for authority along with their habitual raids across the border into England, became such a problem to King James IV of Scotland, that he had 200 Turnbull men arrested. They were commanded to stand before the king wearing only sheets. They had their swords in their hands and halters round their necks. King James then proceeded to randomly hang a number of them and imprison many others in Jedburgh, in an attempt to halt the practice of Border reiving.

Many Turnbull wives were left as widows, and many children were left fatherless on that sad wintery day. Members of the clan around the world solemnly remembered the 15th November 2010, that marked the 500th anniversary of that unhappy day.

The actions of King James caused many Turnbulls to flee the Borders and even leave Scotland permanently. Some went to Ireland. Others went to Europe, where they were employed as mercenary soldiers.

This was followed by a time of peace that lasted for several years, but by 1530, the Turnbulls had rejoined the other Borders clans in their old habit of Reiving. At that time, King James V put a bounty on the head of Borders men with the name of Turnbull and Graham. That resulted in most of the remaining Turnbulls leaving the Borders permanently.

Ferniehirst Castle

On the A6—2 miles south of Jedburgh. Postcode TD8 6NX, (55.4538687, -2.5495584)

Walter Baxter CC SA 2.0

Ferniehirst Castle

The ancestral home of Clan Kerr was built in 1476 by Sir Thomas Kerr as a Borders *pele* (fortified tower) on a hill over the east bank of the Jed Water. Known as Scotland's Frontier Fortress, Ferniehirst's location made it a focus of attacks during the centuries of bloody conflict between England and Scotland. It was repeatedly taken by the English then retaken by the Scots, sometimes with the help of the French. Ferniehirst remained a clan Kerr residence for over 200 years before it fell into decay.

The castle was used by the military during WWII. It was restored to its present condition in 1986 and opened to the public on Heritage Open Days. The castle grounds includes trails that lead along the Jed Water and to a lookout with grand views of the surrounding countryside. The castle itself contains a great hall with a large ornate fireplace and the turret library in the southeast tower. The library, which has a magnificent, carved and painted ceiling, displays books and family mementoes.

Ancrum Moor Battle Site

On the A68—6 miles north of Jedburgh. (55.533640, -2.615132)

The battle site can be seen from the A68, with the mausoleum at the top of the hill, known as Gersit Law to the west of the A68. Lilliards Edge is an uncultivated, partially forested swath that runs northwest at a right angle to the A68 from the mausoleum to a path known as Dere Street, approximately 1/4 mile from the A68. Lilliard's Grave is located at that junction.

Alternately, there is a lovely there-and-back walk around Melrose, that takes the visitor along part of the Roman road of Dere Street. It was also the route used by the English Army to the site of the battle. There are excellent views over the surrounding countryside, including striking views of the distinctive three peaks of the Eildon Hills. This path is on the line of the old Roman road, and it was also the likely route taken by the English.

Monteath Mausoleum is located on top of the hill to the west, known as Gersit Law. This is the hill that the English disastrously charged, in the hope of a quick victory. Once over the stile, keep ahead through the trees to cross over a footpath that leads up to Lilliard's Edge, then to Lilliard's Grave.

Graham Ellis CC SA 2.0

Lady Lilliard's grave

Fair maiden Lilliard lies
under this stane,
Little was her stature,
but great was her fame,
Upon the English loons
she laid many thumps,
And when her legs were
smitten off
she fought upon her stumps.

According to some accounts, it was Lilliard who killed the brutal Sir Ralph Eure. Maid Lilliard was killed in the battle of Ancrum Moor after having both her legs chopped off. The battle site is said to carry the name Lilliard in her honour.

Fatlips Castle

Off the A698—2 miles northeast of Denholm. From Denholm, take the B6405 North for 0.25 mile and turn right (East) onto the first public road after the river. Drive towards Ancrum. At approximately 1.7 miles from the turnoff, on the left, below Fatlips, there is a path in a wooded alleyway between the fields that leads up to Fatlips. The door to the tower is kept locked, but the key is available from Thomas Oliver's Garage in Denholm. Postcode TD9 8SB, (55.4692092, -2.6891652)

Fatlips Castle is a Scottish Borders icon perched atop Minto Crags that looks out over Teviotdale, past Denholm and Bedrule towards England. The famed Rubers Law mountain can be seen, and beyond this, towards the English border. This Borders tower has been known through the centuries as Mantoncrake Castle, Catslick Castle, Minto Castle, and most affectionately as Fatlips Castle.

The origin of the name 'Fatlips' remains a mystery, with a number of proposed sources.

W. Turnbull - CC SA 3.0

Fatlips Castle

There is evidence of an older fort nearby, possibly from the Bronze Age. Little is known of that fort or how the site was likely used during the Roman occupation. The Turnbull Border reivers from the mid-1300s through the 1600s are known to have used the site. In 1375, Walter Turnbull received a charter for the barony of Minto from King David II, son of Robert the Bruce. Walter's son, 'Out with the Swerd' John Turnbull built the first of the second-millennium towers atop Minto Crags towards the end of the 1300s. The tower, which provided a distant view towards England, used bonfires to signal the occupants of Bedrule Castle across the River Teviot to the south, of impending danger.

In 1545, Fatlips Castle was severely destroyed by the Lord Hertford sent by England's King Henry VIII, who was pursuing Mary, Queen of Scots betrothal to his son Edward VI. Sir Gilbert Elliot restored the tower in 1857. The architect, Sir Robert Lorimer, renovated the interior in 1898, as a shooting lodge and private Elliot museum. The building fell into grave disrepair during the late 1900s. In 2013, the exterior was restored with a grant from Historic Scotland.

The entrance to the tower leads to a vaulted basement, with a spiral stair in one corner, giving access to the other two stories and a garret. A round caphouse found at the garret leads to a corbelled parapet. Magnificent views of the Borders and Rubers Law can be seen from the parapet. The tower measures 28 feet from north to south and 32 feet from east to west.

For those who would like to see the Teviotdale from the top on the parapet, please refer to the preceding instructions concerning the key.

Barnhills Castle

Located below (south) and to the east of Fatlips Castle. Follow directions to Fatlips. About halfway up the footpath to Fatlips there is a little-used path to the right (east) that leads to Barnhills. (55.481637, -2.658111

Norman Turnbull

Barnhills Castle

The fourth Turnbull guardian of the Borders was Barnhills Castle, originally known as 'Barne helles.' Barnhills was a small tower house fortification constructed on the Turnbull property below Fatlips Castle. Barnhills was destroyed in 1545 when the English troops invaded and burnt it in the Rough Wooing. In 1548, it was repaired and became known as 'Barnehyll.'

The Castle was appointed to watch over the fords of the Teviot River. The vaulted basement ruins can still be found, with visible evidence of stairs in one corner. The tower once stood around 34 ft by 25 ft, with the entrance facing east towards Craigend Burn.

Carter Bar

On the A68—10 miles south of Jedburgh. This is the border between Scotland and England. (55.354339, -2.477842)

Carter Bar is at the 1,370 foot top of Redesdale in the Cheviot Hills, where the A68 crosses the border of Roxburghshire, Scotland and Northumberland, England.

Colin Smith CC SA 2.0

Carter Bar with the flags of Scotland and Northumberland, England

The boundary line between Scotland and England switched regularly for centuries, until 1018, when the Scottish army of King Malcolm III decisively beat the English Anglo-Saxons at Carham-on-Tweed. The border then took its present position, confirmed by the Treaty of York 1237.

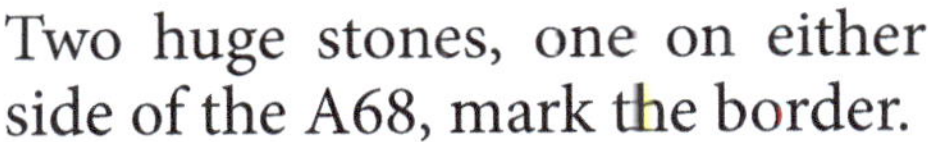

Two huge stones, one on either side of the A68, mark the border.

It is said that in past centuries when smaller markers were used, the Turnbull young men moved the stones and the border a bit to the south every few nights, necessitating the need for immovable rocks.

Standing high up on the Carter Bar in the Cheviot Hills gives a view that takes in the magnificence of the Anglo-Scottish border. This was the location of the gatherings on Truce Days between the leaders the marches in the late Middle Ages.

Kelso

On the A6089—44 miles south of Edinburgh (take A68 to A697 to A6089) / On the A699—12 miles east of the A68 at St. Boswells. Postcode TD5 7AA, (55.600029, -2.432207)

The earliest town of Kelso (originally known as Calkou) emerged from the building of the Abbey, that was completed in 1128. Two town bridges now span the River Tweed in Kelso. Sir Walter Scott attended the Kelso Grammar School in 1783. He once remarked, 'It is the most beautiful if not most the romantic village in Scotland.'

Kelso Abbey

40 Bridge Street in Kelso. Postcode TD5 7JD, (55.597210, -2.432507)

Kelso Abbey was first settled by a community of Monks from France, who had been given a commission in 1128.

Construction began immediately, and by 1143, the abbey was dedicated to the Blessed Virgin and Saint John.

Mick Knapton - CC SA 3.0

Kelso Abbey

Steve Kent - CC 2.0

Ruins of Roxburgh Castle, with Floors Castle in the background

Roxburgh Castle

On the A698—12 miles east of the A68, A68 to A698 at Bonjedward, to Roxburgh Street, Kelso, Signs to Floors Castle. Postcode TD5 7RW (55.604851, -2.459865)

Roxburgh Castle was built in 1128 at the junction of the rivers Teviot and Tweed as a primary defence during the reign of King David I. The castle fell into English hands in 1174 and was retaken by the Scots in 1314. Subsequently, it changed hands several times until the Scots destroyed both the castle and Roxburgh town in 1460 to prevent either from ever falling into English hands again. King James II was killed at Roxburgh Castle during the 1460 siege.

Very little of the castle stonework walls remain to this day. What does remain, sits opposite Floors, on the grounds of Floors Castle.

Floors Castle

On the A698—12 miles east of the A68, A68 to A698 at Bonjedward, to Roxburgh Street, Kelso, signs to Floors Castle. Postcode TD5 7RW (55.604851, -2.459865)

Mihael Grmek - CC 3.0

The lands of Floors belonged to the monks of Kelso Abbey, until the Reformation, when these lands were given to Robert Ker of Cessford, later the first Earl of Roxburgh, by King James VI.

Despite its name, Floors Castle is a country house, not a fortress. It was built in the 1720s by the architect William Adam for Duke John Ker, on the site of an earlier Borders tower house. In the 19th century, the architect William Playfair added decorative turrets and battlements for Duke James Innes-Ker. Floors is Scotland's largest inhabited Castle and one of the leading visitor attractions in the Scottish Borders.

Floors Castle is now a Category A listed building. Its grounds, listed in the inventory of Gardens and Designed Landscapes; the national listing of significant gardens in Scotland, are open to the public.

Hume Castle

Off the B6404—12 miles east of the A68 at St. Boswells, A68 to B6404 9 miles to B6364 3 miles. Postcode TD5 7TW, (55.665169, -2.470937)

Hume Castle, built in the 1200s, is said to have been one of the most formidable defensive castles in the eastern Borders. It was expanded and strengthened in the 1540s with the help of the French military, with added ramparts and artillery platforms. The French influence can be seen in the appearance of the castle that does not resemble any other of the Borders fortifications.

Though nothing remains of it now, there was initially a village on the south slope of the castle.

James Denham - CC 2.0

Hume Castle

In spite of its considerable strength, the English army under the Duke of Somerset, captured Hume castle in 1547. The Scots recaptured it in a night attack in 1549 with the help of spies who infiltrated the English defenders. Hume Castle was again taken by the English in 1569, only to be recaptured by the Scots in 1572.

The end of the castle's military life came in 1651 when it stood against Cromwell's invading army. Though the castle resisted the artillery bombardment quite well, the defenders eventually surrendered, and Cromwell's troops blew up the castle.

In 1770, Hugh Hume-Campbell, 3rd Earl of Marchmont, bought the site and had the walls that are still visible today re-built. With its excellent vantage point, the new castle was used as a lookout and beacon station during the Napoleonic Wars. On the night of 31st January 1804, the sentry mistook the fire of some charcoal burners in the Cheviot Hills for the French army. The beacon of Hume Castle was lit resulting in the Great Alarm of 1804, as thousands of volunteers mustered to fight off French invaders that didn't exist.

Duns

On the B6456—19 miles east of the A68 at Lauder (take A68 to A697 to B6456). Postcode TD11 3AA, (55.777794, -2.343461)

The Iron Age fort on top of Duns Law and the remains of huts within it indicate the domestic and military use of Duns during the Iron Age.

Because of its location along a main road, Duns was frequently attacked by the English in border raids and as they headed north. Sir James Douglas and Sir Thomas Randolph gathered their armies at Duns in 1318 when they organised to recapture Berwick from the English. In 1333, Sir Archibald Douglas gathered his troops at Duns before marching on Berwick to relieve its siege by the English. He was defeated at the Battle of Halidon Hill, and William Turn-e-bull was killed.

When the Earl of Northumberland invaded Scotland in 1377, he camped at Duns. During the night, the inhabitants of the town attacked the invaders in the battle of Duns, making a great deal of noise with the rattles used locally to scare birds away from the crops. The townsmen routed the confused English force. That Battle of Duns is the source of the town's motto, 'Duns dings a!'

The original Castle of Duns would appear to have been built by Randolph Earl of Moray in 1320 following a grant of the lands of Duns by his uncle, Robert the Bruce.

Duns Castle

Off the A6105—1/2 mile north of Duns. Postcode TD11 3NW, (55.782263, -2.355913)

Duns Castle was originally a Borders pele tower, built in 1320 by Randolph Earl of Moray, a nephew of King Robert the Bruce.

Rich Tea - CC 2.0

The Covenanters gathered their forces at Duns Castle in 1639, to resist Charles I's religious reforms and fight for freedom of worship.

The castle has been the seat of the Hay family since the 17th century and was converted into a Gothic style castle in 1818. It is currently a historic house and private residence at the centre of a beautiful 1200 acre estate, including a publicly accessible park with two small man-made lakes; the 'Hen Poo' and 'Mill Dam.'

Smailholm Tower

Off the B6404—6 miles east of the A68 / 7 miles west of Kelso. (55.604328, -2.576164)

Smailholm Tower was constructed in the 15th century by the Pringles as a defensive Borders tower. The lands of Smailholm belonged to Sir James (Black) Douglas, who likely gave or entrusted the tower area to the Pringles for defence. The name comes from the old English *smail* (small) and *holm* (little island).

Dave Souzaa - CC 2.5

The original tower, the centre of a small community, was surrounded by a barmkin wall, in which stood cottages, a chapel, mill, and enclosures for farm animals. Traces of those can still be seen. Close to the tower, there are old earthworks which suggest an earlier settlement from around the first millennium BC.

Like most Borders towers, the English raided Smailholm repeatedly. In 1546, troops from Wark Castle in Northumberland England sacked the tower taking prisoners and cattle.

In 1645, Sir William Scott of Harde purchased Smailholm and rebuilt parts of the tower and barmkin. The tower measured approximately 40 feet by 31 feet and had four storeys. The walls were almost 8 feet thick at the base and had a stone flag roof.

The tower provided inspiration to Sir Walter Scott, who lived there with his paternal grandfather for a period, reportedly for the benefit of his health. It was during that time that he developed his love for the ballads of the Scottish Borders. Smailholm provides the setting for Scott's ballad, 'The Eve of St. John.'

The upper three floors of Smailholm Tower are now a museum, displaying costumed figures and tapestries that recall Scott's ballads and the tower's turbulent history.

Eyemouth

On the A1—9 miles north of Berwick-upon-Tweed. Postcode TD14 5AA, (55.869058, -2.091068)

Eyemouth, the seventh largest town in the Borders, is so named because it sits at the mouth of the Eye Water River on the North Sea. Berwick-upon-Tweed is now a part of England, while nearby Eyemouth is the easternmost town of these Borders Trails.

Eyemouth has always been home to fishermen, including William Spears, the town hero who is celebrated by a bronze statue in Eyemouth Market Place, pointing the way to Ayton, where he began his successful revolt against the tithes (taxes) on fish levied by the Church.

Eyemouth Harbour

The town is also known for the Eyemouth Disaster of 14th October 1881, when most of its fishing fleet; some 20 boats and 129 fishermen were lost in a terrible storm. A famous tapestry housed in the Eyemouth Museum depicts this event.

Fort Point

In Eyemouth, the point of land on the water just beyond the caravan park. Postcode TD14 5BE, (55.873988, -2.094035)

This promontory holds the first *trace Italienne* style fortification in Britain. It was constructed in 1547 by invading English troops and in 1557 by French troops supporting the Scottish king. Two lines of ramparts with their gun emplacements that can still be made out in the grass-covered mounds. The point also provides an excellent view of the cliffs and nesting seabirds.

Pinkie Cleugh Battle Site

On the A1—6 miles south of Edinburgh in Musselburgh. Postcode EH21 6RY, (55.933797, -3.049306)

The Battle of Pinkie Cleugh took place on the banks of the River Esk in 1547, as part of the Rough Wooing. It was the last of the formal pitched battles between the English and Scottish armies. It ended as a severe defeat for the Scots and became known as Black Saturday.

Kim Traynor - CC 3.0

River Esk and Inveresk Church at Musselburgh

There is a plaque, that has the battle details on the south side of the bridge over the River Esk.

Despite being in what is now a built-up area, close to the eastern suburbs of Edinburgh it is a surprisingly rural walk. An attractive path beside the river Esk changes quickly from the town centre of Musselburgh into greener and quieter surroundings to much of the battle site, which is still open country. The views extend from Falside Hill, where the English army was camped, to the distinctive bulk of Arthurs Seat in Holyrood Park and along the coast to the Firth of Forth.

The main battlefield is now cultivated land a half mile southeast of Inveresk church just past the railroad. The English position can be seen from Fa'side Castle looking out towards the Firth of Forth. The Scottish position can be seen from the Musselburgh golf course, that sits between the B6415 and a bend in the River Esk. The centre of the Scottish position was to the left of the clubhouse.

Along the south side of the river, there is a footpath that leads through part of the battle area, providing not only a pleasant walk but a good perspective of the terrain.

The old Roman bridge is at the eastern end of the River Esk Path. Despite being called the 'Roman bridge', it is a medieval structure and was for many years, the only bridge across the river. At the Battle of Pinkie, it was controlled by the Scots and protected by artillery

Callum Black - CC 2.0

Innerwick Castle

On the A1—30 miles east of Edinburgh. Follow A1 27 miles to East Lothian. Exit to Innerwick. Follow directions to Innerwick Castle Barns Ness Terrace, Dunbar. Postcode EH42 1QT, (55.955435, -2.425511)

The dramatic remains of Innerwick Castle are perched on top of a sandstone outcrop, almost facing Thornton Castle across the ravine. The original fortress was built by the Stewarts in the 1300s and passed to the Hamiltons in 1398.

Part of the history of Innerwick is unusual in that it was attacked in 1403 by joint forces of mortal enemies; the English knight (Hotspur) Percy and Archibald (Black) Douglas, as part of their united, but failed revolt against Henry IV of England.

Like most Borders strongholds Innerwick and neighbouring Home (Hume) Thornton Castle was attacked in 1547, during the Rough Wooing. The Hamiltons barricaded the doors and fought from the battlements. The castle was set ablaze, and attackers stormed in killing all of the defenders but one, who jumped from the battlements into the ravine 60 feet below. The English commander was so impressed by this feat of daring, that he ordered the man's life to be spared. Unfortunately, the soldiers attacking Thornton Castle did not hear the order and killed him.

The useful life of Innerwick Castle came to an end along with most other Borders stone fortresses, when they were used in an attempt to defend against Cromwell's New Model Army in the Wars of the Three Kingdoms. No fortress could withstand the bombardment of modern cannons and mortars. The very nature of war changed and it became economically impractical to build or repair such castles. Accessible parts of the castle served as a stone quarry for farm and cottage walls.

Fa'side Castle

Off the A1—10 miles east of Edinburgh. A1 (9 miles) to A6094 (Salters Road) south. Take the first (unnamed) road to the left (east) off of Salters Road and drive 1.4 mi to the castle. Post Code EH33 2LE, (55.927900, -2.9975).

Greig Brash - CC 3.0

Fa'side Castle is named for the Fawside family who owned it from the late 14th century, though it began as an earlier fortified tower built by Saer de Quincy, Earl of Winchester in 1189. Sir William Douglas attacked the castle during the first War of Scottish Independence. After his 1306 rebellion, King Robert the Bruce seized the castle and gave it to the Setons.

In 1371, the Setons sold the castle to the Fawsides whose family owned it for the next 260 years.

Fa'side Castle and its occupants were burned by the English in the wake of their victory in the Battle of Pinkie Cleugh in 1547. Fa'side was rebuilt and expanded. Mary, Queen of Scots, stayed there on 14th June 1567, on her way to the Battle of Carberry Hill.

Dirleton Castle

On the A198—22 miles east of Edinburgh. A1 to A198 to B1377 (Main Road) to Castle Park, Post Code: EH39 5ER, (56.045914, -2.77815).

A Medieval reminder of the 13th-century stone castles, this Dirleton was built as a fortress in 1240, to guard the coastal approach to Edinburgh from English invasions. It is one of Scotland's oldest strongholds. The castle was heavily damaged in the Wars of Scottish Independence.

Jonathan Oldenbuck - CC 3.0

Only the original *donjon* (keep) remains intact, forming the southwest part of Dirleton Castle today. Visitors can view the castle buildings and enjoy its magnificent gardens.

Hailes Castle

Off the A1—16 miles east of Edinburgh. A1 to A199 to Braehead Loan Road. Postcode EH41 4PY, (55.9731498, -2.6849985)

Originally built as a tower house, Hailes Castle stands on a promontory along the banks of the Tyne River, and in its day effectively controlled the routes to Edinburgh. Mary, Queen of Scots, lived at Hailes for a time.

Supergolden - CC 3.0

North face of Hailes Castle

In 1400, Hailes Castle withstood a massive attack from Henry (Hotspur) Percy of Northumberland, England.

The attackers were ultimately defeated in a counter-attack led by Archibald Douglas. Three years later it was successfully besieged by Archibald Dunbar, followed by a massacre of the castle's inhabitants.

Halidon Hill Battle Site

Off the A1—53 miles southeast of Edinburgh. A1 (52 miles) to A6105 Duns Rd (1.5 miles)—near Berwick-upon Tweed, England. (55.7864074, -2.0423305)

The Battle of Halidon Hill took place on a hill outside Berwick-upon-Tweed on the 19th July 1333. It was there that the first Turnbull, William Turn-e-bull (Will-'o-Rule) died in battle.

Just over the current national border, the sloped terrain rises to 600 feet. There is a small monument on the roadside commemorating the battle and an information board outlaying the battleground in the car park.

The battlefield walk offers the visitor good access to the battle site.

Kenneth Turnbull

Halidon Hill Battle marker

From the top of Halidon Hill, visitors can look down on the ancient town of Berwick-upon-Tweed.

Dunbar Castle and Site of Dunbar Battles

Off the A1—30 miles east of Edinburgh. A1 (23 miles) to A199 (.4 mile) to A1087 (7 miles). Postcode EH42 1ET, (56.001182, -2.52074).

Phillip Capper - CC 3.0

Dunbar Castle and harbour

The remains of Dunbar Castle stand atop a rocky outcrop projecting into the Firth of Forth. The castle has a turbulent history having been attacked on many occasions. A fortification is known to have occupied that spot at least since Roman times when, as a timber fort, it was occupied by the Votanidi tribe. The Picts later occupied the site, though little is known about that period.

In AD 849, Kenneth MacAlpin was listed as the owner, having dispatched his competitors to become king of both Picts and Gaels. It is believed that he used the fortress to defend against the Viking raids of that period.

Dunbar Castle developed from a Dark Ages fort into a medieval castle that has witnessed no less than three battles between the English and the Scots. The earliest was a field battle in 1296, during the Wars of Scottish Independence. It was an English reprisal against the Scottish king, John Balliol and became a decisive English victory. The second was a sea battle, that occurred in 1489, with a Scottish victory. The third battle took place in 1650. This was a field battle, known as the Third English Civil War that ended as a decisive English Parliamentarian victory.

The Dunbar Castle and Battle site have magnificent sweeping views over Dunbar, the East Lothian coast and the location of the battles. There is also information about the battles in the Townhouse Museum in Dunbar.

Outside Borders

Stirling

Once the capital of Scotland, Stirling is visually dominated by the royal citadel of Stirling Castle. The city is known as the Gateway to the Highlands. It has been said, 'Stirling, like a huge brooch, clasps Highlands and Lowlands together.'

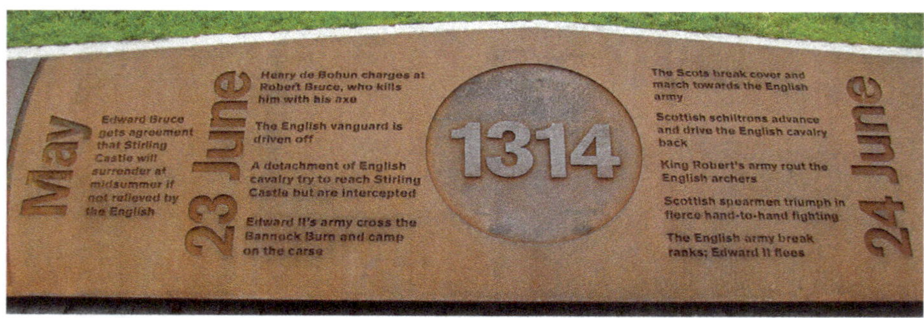

Kenneth Turnbull

Bannockburn Battle Site Visitor Centre

Take the M80/M9 and exit on the A872 towards Stirling—Glasgow Road, Whins Of Milton, Stirling. Postcode FK7 0LJ, (56.092664, -3.934128)

Because of the importance of the Battle of Bannockburn to the history of the nation of Scotland, this site is one of the major Scottish attractions. It is within easy reach of both Edinburgh and Glasgow.

There is an open area where the battle occurred with a large statue of King Robert the Bruce. The museum includes a 3D exhibit.

Falkirk Battle Site

Off the M9—14 miles southeast of Stirling—M9 12 miles southeast to A905 1/2 mile south to A904 1/2 mile southwest to A9 1/4 mile south to B805 1/4 mile south—Callendar Park is a vast area of wooded parkland near the centre of Falkirk. (55.987885 -3.763493)

The exact site where the battle of Falkirk took place is not known for certain. Various sites around the modern town of Falkirk have been suggested, including the area of Callendar Park.

There is a good sized car park near the entrance to Callendar Park. Visitors can begin the walk along the tarred walkway, that starts past the yellow vehicle barrier. The route is lined by some magnificent mature trees and passes close to a cairn that commemorates the 1298 Battle of Falkirk. William Wallace was beaten in this battle, by the army of King Edward I.

The Falkirk Memorial Cairn in the park commemorates this 1298 battle.

The 14th-century Callendar House contains a section of the Antonine Wall and a museum with exhibits of the Battle of Falkirk and the Antonine Wall.

Sean Mack - CC SA 2.5

The Falkirk Wheel features modern technology, but is an excellent reason to visit Falkirk. It is the world's first and only rotating boat lift. This engineering marvel transports boats 115 feet between the levels of the Union, and Forth and Clyde canals. One can take a ride on the wheel or learn more about it at the Visitor Centre.

Stirling Castle

Off the M9—48 miles northwest of Edinburgh, on Castle Esplanade in Stirling. Castle Esplanade, Stirling. Postcode FK8 1EJ, (56.123790, -3.947428)

Finlay McWalter - CC SA 3.0

Built on a large rocky outcrop of a quartz-dolerite intrusion that is locally known as 'Castle Hill,' Stirling Castle has one of the most important strategic locations in Scotland.

The plateau of Stirling Castle was a Pictish stronghold as early as the second century and was likely inhabited for 2,000 years before that. It has been recorded that in 1110, King Alexander I built a chapel on the site, indicating that a fortification may have existed.

After the Battle of Bannockburn, the original castle was destroyed on the orders of King Robert the Bruce. This was so that the English could no longer use it against him, as it had witnessed the major battles of Stirling Bridge and Bannockburn. The oldest part of the present castle was not built until 1381 after William Wallace and King Robert the Bruce had died. The task of rebuilding the castle began under King David II when the Wars of independence had ended in 1356.

Over many generations, European royalty gave diplomatic gifts of lions. In the 1500s, King James V may well have kept a lion at the Stirling Castle as a living symbol of Scottish royalty. King David, King James III, and King James IV all owned lions.

Through the Middle Ages and the period of the Renaissance, Stirling was regarded as the most important royal castle and entertained the royal court of Stewart Scotland at the peak of their history. Several Scottish kings and queens were crowned at Stirling Castle, including the infant Mary, Queen of Scots. It was also the birthplace of James III and the childhood days of James V.

Over time, the castle suffered eight sieges; the last one being in 1746 when Bonnie Prince Charlie was unsuccessful in his attempts to recapture it.

Visitors to Stirling Castle with its many buildings will be able to catch a glimpse into an earlier lifestyle, including the Great Hall, the large tapestries, and a museum. Other attractions include the Queen Anne Gardens, the Great Kitchens and Argyll's Lodging, the oldest surviving 17th-century town-house.

Stirling Bridge Battle Site

Stirling Bridge crosses the River Forth from Bridgehaugh Road in Stirling. (56.128618, -3.936816)

Snapshots of the Past - CC SA 2.0

The picturesque Old Stirling Bridge is still used for pedestrian traffic

The site of the original Stirling Bridge lies about 180 yards upstream from this reconstructed bridge. The battle that took place at Stirling Bridge was a decisive victory for the Scots led by William Wallace during the First War of Independence in 1297.

William Wallace Monument

Off the A91—Abbey Craig, Hillfoots Road, Stirling. Postcode FK9 5LF (56.138769, -3.9179638)

The William Wallace Monument is a 219-foot verticle tower on the summit of Abbey Craig. It was from this point that William Wallace reputedly watched the army of King Edward I before his successful battle at nearby Stirling Bridge.

There are several artefacts, which belonged to William Wallace, including his large two-handed sword.

Finlay McWalter - CC SA 3.0

Visitors can access the monument by choosing an invigorating uphill walk to the summit or be driven by regular departures on a free minibus shuttle from the car park to the monument.

Caerlaverock Castle

Off the A75—38 miles northeast of Carlisle, England in Dumfries and Galloway, Southwest Scotland—M6 10 miles north to A75, 18 miles west to B725, then 10 miles west. Postcode DG1 4RU, (54.9756934, -3.5240488)

Built by Sir John Maxwell from 1220 onwards, Caerlaverock Castle with its wide moat, twin-towered gatehouse, and picturesque battlements, is a classic example of a medieval castle fortress built for this period. The triangular shape of its great walls is unique in all of Britain. Caerlaverock Castle, situated close to the English border, controlled the important waterways of the Solway and the River Nith; the southwestern gateways to medieval Scotland.

F. Simon Ledingham - CC SA 2 0

Caerlaverock Castle

In July 1300, King Edward I, nicknamed 'Longshanks' because of his height and known as the 'Hammer of the Scots' for his brutality, attacked Caerlaverock with around 100 knights and 3,000 soldiers. His weapons included the Warwolf, believed to be the largest trebuchet ever made, capable of hurling 200 lb stones up to 1300 feet. The Maxwells clan defending the castle, repelled the attackers numerous times, but in the end, they were forced to surrender, after which it was found that only sixty Scots had fought off multiple attacks by the whole English army.

That may have been the most famous siege of Caerlaverock Castle, but it was not to be the last. The castle was besieged in 1356 by Scottish forces and then in 1544 and 1570 by the English.

Glasgow

University of Glasgow

University Avenue, Glasgow. Postcode G12 8QQ, (55.8721211, -4.2903892)

William Turnbull, who was born in Bedrule, founded the University in Glasgow in 1451. He studied at St. Andrews University and several continental universities, before becoming a leading minister of King James II of Scotland and holding the office of Keeper of the Privy Seal. William also had a successful career in the church, becoming the Archdeacon of St. Andrews, the king's agent at the Papal Court, and finally, as Bishop of Glasgow.

The University of Glasgow was granted a charter or papal bull from Pope Nicholas V, at the request of King James II. The bull gave Bishop William Turnbull authority to add a university to the

Glasgow Cathedral. This is the second oldest university in Scotland after St. Andrews and the fourth oldest university in the English speaking world. The university was designed after the University of Bologna, where Pope Nicholas had been a student. Bishop Turnbull was a graduate of St. Andrews University.

University of Glasgow main gates the with names of James II, Turnbull, and other University luminaries

University Mace with Turnbull arms (bottom centre)

In December 1453, William Turnbull granted to members of the university the right of trading within the town, without payment of custom. He also authorised the rector to act as a judge in civil and pecuniary cases and the less serious disagreements between members of the university or between them and the citizens of the bishop's territory. The more serious cases were set aside for the Bishop's Court. William Turnbull died while visiting Rome in 1454.

The University of Glasgow mace is engraved with the Turnbull arms of the founder. The university gates carry the names of James II, Turnbull, and other famous figures of the university. There are several other images and references to William Turnbull throughout the University.

Bothwell Castle

10 miles southeast of Glasgow—M8, 8 miles east to M73, 1 mile south to A721 1/4 mile east to B7071 1 mile to Castle Avenue, Bothwell, Uddingston. Postcode G71 8BL, (55.809453, -4.094925).

The ancestors of Clan Murray originally constructed Bothwell Castle in 1252, on a steep bank of the River Clyde, 10 miles south of Glasgow in South Lanarkshire. As a medieval castle, its purpose was to guard a strategic crossing of the Clyde River. Before long, it was to play an essential part in the Wars of Scottish Independence. A large cylindrical *donjon* (fortified tower or inner keep) had been constructed earlier, but before the castle was completed, the tower was severely damaged through a series of sieges by the English.

When Edward I (Longshanks) invaded Scotland in 1296, Bothwell Castle was one of his first targets. He captured the castle and William Moray, the son of Baron Walter Moray who owned the castle. Thanks to a massive effort in a siege lasting 14 months, the Scots won the castle back in 1298.

Otter - CC SA 3.0

In 1301, the English King Edward I with over 6,000 troops, returned to South Lanarkshire and using siege engines, recaptured Bothwell Castle. The English garrison held out in the castle against Robert the Bruce until 1314.

Northumberland

Battle of Otterburn Battle Site

On the A696—about 1 mile west of Otterburn, Northumberland (55.236195, -2.195369)

The Battle of Otterburn was fought by moonlight during the night of 19th August 1388, between a Scottish force under Sir James Douglas and a much larger English army under Sir Henry (Hotspur) Percy. The battle was a Scottish victory.

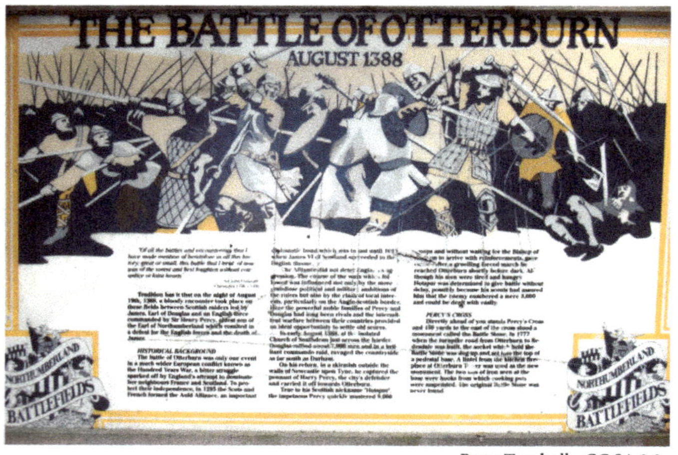

Battle of Otterburn monument information board

About a mile west of Otterburn, there is a Percy Cross monument, erected in 1777, that sits in a small wooded area next to the A696. There is a sign on the road marking the site. The farmland battlefield appears as it may have looked over six centuries ago. There is not a great deal to see at the site, but it does give cause for reflection with a drive through the Northumberland countryside that is both striking and scenic.

Flodden Field

Off the A698—15 miles southwest of Berwick-upon-Tweed, England. Take the A698 southwest 11 miles to A697 southeast 1.5 miles, turn right (southeast) towards Branxton, follow signs to Flodden Field carpark. Postcode TD12 4SN, (55.6315484, -2.1867205)

This battlefield is the site of the largest battle between the two kingdoms, where the army of King James IV of Scotland and the English Earl of Surrey fought on the 9th September 1513. The main battle took place on the slopes of Branxton Hill, to the south of Branxton Village. King James and as many as 10,000 of his followers were killed in his loss to the English.

This conflict began when King Henry VIII claimed to be the overlord of Scotland. This dictate angered the Scots, and as a reaction, King James IV declared war on England in support of the Auld Alliance with France. This was aimed at diverting the English troops from their campaign against the French, under King Louis XII.

This site is arguably the most evocative, informative, and accessible of the battle sites in Northumbria and the Scottish Borders. Its location provides the atmosphere, with a battle monument that overlooks the now tranquil landscape; empty rolling hills, magnificent and extensive views, with a few sounds of the birds and the rustling of the wind.

The Flodden battlefield is marked by a granite cross and a public battlefield trail that leads through the heart of the battle site along the lanes, permissive paths and public footpaths that are punctuated by information boards. The walk starts by heading over Branxton Hill and then on to Flodden Edge. There is some climbing, and you can expect a few overgrown stretches on some of the cross-field paths.

Paul Barlow - CC SA 3.0

Flodden memorial cross

The building today is mainly of the Victorian era, but it was thanks to its medieval predecessors, that many of the bodies, both English and Scottish, were brought after the carnage of the battle. Additional information is available at nearby Etal Castle.

Solway Moss Battlefield

Off the A7—8 miles north or Carlisle in Longtown, A7 north 7 miles to Arthuret Road, .5 mile south to Saint Michael's church carpark. Postcode CA6 5SH, (54.999388, -2.971193)

When Henry VIII of England broke from the Roman Catholic Church, he asked his nephew King James V of Scotland, to follow suit. King James refused to even meet with Uncle Henry to discuss this matter. Henry VIII was used to having his way, so he sent his army against Scotland.

They clashed in the heart of the Debatable Lands. This was the territory between the Eden and Esk bordering the Solway Firth, that had been fought over for centuries by the English and Scottish lords.

With the Scottish army officers squabbling over leadership, morale was low and the troops in disarray, even before the battle. In the battle that ensued, they broke rank quickly and were routed by a much smaller English force. Few soldiers were killed in battle, but a large number of the Scots drowned in the Esk River as they fled.

Many, including the leaders Lord Robert Maxwell and Lord Oliver Sinclair, were taken prisoner.

Norman Turnbull

The River Esk, deeper at the time, caused most of the casualties as the Scottish troops attempted to escape.

St. Michael's churchyard lies approximately where the Scots lined up at the start of the battle. In the early 17th century, the church building replaced the one that stood during the battle. As you walk across the churchyard, there are grand views across to the Solway and Esk valley and to the line of the Southern Uplands.

Longtown, which developed two hundred years after the battle, sits on the northern part of the battlefield. The landscape has changed significantly since then when it was just a boggy moor. Unfortunately, there is no monument to this battle. Notwithstanding the changes, the terrain and views can still be appreciated, as one considers how the Battle of Solway Moss paved the way for a United Kingdom.

Hadrian's Wall

Segedunum site is off the A1—66 miles south of Berwick-upon-Tweed. A1 53 miles south to A19 12 miles south to A187 (Hadrian Road) .5 mile west to Segedunum. Buddle St, Wallsend, England. Postcode NE28 6HR, (54.988494, -1.531237).

A considerable portion of Hadrian's Wall still stands today and remains as a popular tourist attraction. The wall construction was initially 80 Roman miles long, which in current measurements, is 73 miles.

There are many viewing points to visit the wall; the Northumberland National Park, Walltown, Cawfields Steel Rig, Brocoitia, Housesteads, and Wallsend. However, one of the best viewing places is Segedunum (Strong Fort) at Wallsend, in Northumberland.

Velella - CC SA 3.0

Hadrian's wall near Cawfields quarry, Northumberland

Segedunum was at the eastern end of Hadrian's Wall near the banks of the River Tyne at the North Sea. The original purpose of Segedunum is not certain. There are theories that it was to keep the barbarians from the north out of England and as a frontier post for trade, to control immigration, stop smuggling, or provide customs taxation. Perhaps all of those reasons apply.

Kenneth Turnbull

Hadrian's Wall at Hosesteads Fort

Built in 127AD, Segedunum was used as a Roman garrison for almost 300 years up to the end of the 5th century. This most thoroughly excavated fort on Hadrian's Wall, enables visitors to see foundations of the original fort, a reconstructed Roman military bathhouse, a museum, an observation tower, and a portion of the original wall.

Carlisle Castle

Off the A7 44 miles south of Hawick, A7 south 42 miles to Castle Way, 2 miles west. Postcode CA3 8UR, (54.8975096, -2.9421404).

Carlisle Castle in Carlisle city centre, Cumbria, England

Ten miles south of the Scottish border town of Gretna, at the head of Solway Firth, Carlisle was initially established by the Romans as a centre from which supplies and support were provided to the forts and posts along Hadrian's Wall. The town grew and continued as an important military centre for Scotland, until William the Conqueror's son, William Rufus, won the region and made it part of England in 1091.

Carlisle Castle was built in 1093 and once served as a prison for Mary, Queen of Scots. Over time, the castle has witnessed many wars and invasions due to its proximity to the border. The Castle still stands quite intact today and houses the Border Regiment Museum.

King Henry I of England gave the authority for the laying of the Priory foundation in the early 12th century. The Priory later became Carlisle Cathedral. The town of Carlisle featured often in the struggle for power throughout the battles with William Wallace and King Robert the Bruce against King Edward III of England.

Today, Carlisle a vibrant town of around 100,000 inhabitants, is the primary cultural, commercial and industrial centre for north Cumbria in England. Besides its castle, the city has several museums and heritage centres. Carlisle provides a worthy and useful taste of England for visitors to the Scottish Borders.

Beyond Borders

Large numbers of Scots from the Borders emigrated to Northern Ireland, USA, Canada, England, Australia, New Zealand, South Africa, and other nations in smaller numbers.

W. Turnbull - CC SA 3.0

Ever since the union of the crowns of Scotland and England in 1603, persecution or prosecution, depending on one's point of view, of the Borders people became common as King James VI/I attempted to change their previously accepted practice of reiving. Many families changed their names to avoid prosecution. Turnbull became, Trimble, Trumbull, Trumble and so on. Others emigrated, especially to Ireland and the New World. This resulted in a steady depopulation of the Borders. It also resulted in a strong Scottish influence on the culture and politics of the nations where they made their new lives.

Ireland

The Scottish lords, James Hamilton and Hugh Montgomery, used their connections to King James VI/I to obtain vast tracts of land in County Down, Ireland. Beginning in 1603, they recruited large numbers of tenant farmers to settle in Ulster by offering low rents. The venture was successful financially for Hamilton and Montgomery and as well, providing a better life for their tenants.

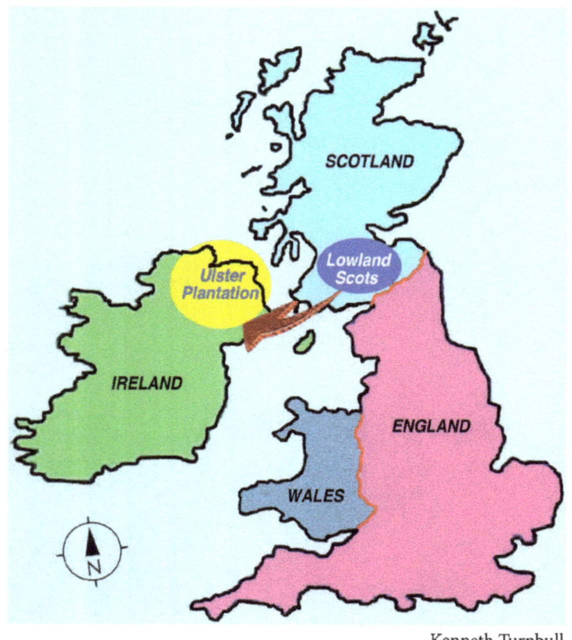

Kenneth Turnbull

The Ulster Plantation Plan, Ireland 1609

There were many reasons why the Scots moved to Ulster. For most, it was with a hope that they would find a new and better life for themselves and their families. The younger sons of landowners saw the opportunity to acquire their own estates. Farmers hoped to receive larger and better farms. Landless labourers hoped they would have their own farms rather than having to work for others.

So successful was this initial venture that King James chartered several additional settlements including the Virginia Company in 1606, the Ulster Plantation of 1610 and the Nova Scotia Charter of 1621. These drew large numbers of people from the Borders. The Scottish immigrants in Ireland became known as 'Ulster-Scots.'

Ulster was the last province in Ireland to be brought under English control. King James hoped that the planting of loyal subjects would stop the threat of rebellion. Keeping law and order in Ulster was expensive, and the king was also worried that if a Spanish army invaded Ireland, they would find support among the Irish.

King James hoped that the people, who immigrated to Ulster during the time of the Plantation, would help him change the province. He expected that settlers from both England and Scotland would sopport him and his government. In the king's mind, Ulster needed to be developed more like England and Scotland. Most of the Irish people living in Ulster did not agree and resented the king's meddlesome methods in their land.

In the 18th century, the Ulster-Scots, known abroad as Scots-Irish began to emigrate out of Ireland in large numbers. The term Ulster-Scots tends to be used in the British Isles, while abroad they are known as Scots-Irish. Having moved once already and broken the link with their ancestral home in Scotland, it was quite easy and practical to move again where a better future could be had.

Emigration directly from Scotland also continued through the 18th and 19th centuries, but so many arrived from Ireland that the Scottish and Scots-Irish were virtually indistinguishable.

North America

Rosedown Plantation in St. Francisville, Louisiana, United States. Built in 1835 by cotton planters Daniel and Martha Turnbull

The earliest Scot to visit North America was a Christian bard (professional storyteller) from the Hebrides who accompanied the Viking explorer, Bjami Herjolfsson around 985 AD.

But it took another 25 years before the first Scots landed on American soil. Records indicate that two slaves, a Scotsman Haki and a woman named Hekja, were among the Leif Erikson party who explored America. Erikson, an Icelandic explorer, is regarded as being the first European to land on the continent.

The Scottish slaves were used in searching for and gathering grain and grapes. The native grapes in particular (to which Vinland was named) were from an area, which is now known as New Brunswick.

Kenneth Turnbull

Ships similar to this used for the colonisation of America. The *Sparrow Hawk*, carrying 20 passengers was wrecked off the American coast in 1626.

It was another 500 years before Christopher Columbus arrived on the shores of North America. Jamestown, the earliest permanent English settlement, was established 600 years later in 1607.

In 1620, pilgrims on the *Mayflower* sailed to the eastern coast of North America when storms forced them to land in the coastal shoals of Provincetown Harbour after 67 days at sea. While anchored there, they wrote and signed a democratic document, known as the 'Mayflower Compact,' a social contract governing their actions for survival in the new land. On board the *Mayflower* was an early Scottish immigrant, Robert Sprout, who worked his way to pay for his passage.

In time, thirteen colonies were established along the Atlantic coast of North America. Scottish emigrants were welcomed and settled in these colonies: Virginia, Connecticut, Pennsylvania, Maryland, Rhode Island, New Hampshire, South Carolina, New York, Delaware, New Jersey, Georgia, Massachusetts and North Carolina.

In 1717, the British Transportation Act of Parliament was passed, whereby criminals could be transported to North America for indentured service, as punishment in lieu of execution. These prisoners were placed into a bond service for a period of 7 years for minor crimes and 14 years for crimes of a more serious nature. The Transportation Act also allowed merchants and others to contract with willing 15-20 year-olds to be transported and serve up to eight years of indentured service. Around 50,000 men, women, and children were transported to the colonies in this manner.

From 1739 to 1752, the Governor of North Carolina offered tax–exempt land grants to Scots, in a bid to have them settle in that colony.

After the Catholic Scots, led by Bonnie Prince Charlie, were defeated at the Battle of Culloden in 1746, many Scots immigrated into the thirteen colonies, but in particular, Virginia and South Carolina.

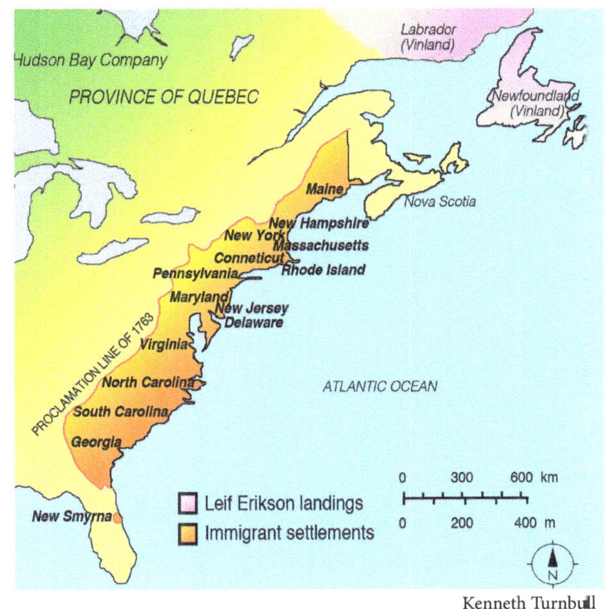

Kenneth Turnbull

Early colonies of the Americas, where around 50,000 Scots settled between 1763 and 1776

Included in the early colonial settlements, was New Smyrna, Florida. In 1773, Scottish born Dr Andrew Turnbull established an agricultural settlement he named 'Smyrnea.' The agricultural venture failed, but most of the settlers remained. One of Dr Turnbull's sons went from New Smyrna to Mexico, where he became the forefather of a large extended Mexican Turnbull family.

After winning independence from England in 1783, the United States of America rapidly underwent an industrial revolution in the 19th century. This resulted in a demand for cheap labour and an influx of Scottish workers, especially to the cities. During this same period, Canada lured many Scots to Ontario (then Upper Canada) and westward with large grants of land.

Nova Scotia

King James granted a charter for a settlement in Acadia, which he called Nova Scotia (New Scotland), to Earl William Alexander of Stirling in 1621. Acadia officially remained a French colony until 1710, when the British conquered it.

Joanne Baker

Tribute to the Scottish Settlers Monument

Makaristos - CC SA 3.0

Scottish Flag of Nova Scotia

Scottish immigrants established a settlement at Charlesfort, near Port Royal, and at Rosemar, on Cape Breton Island. From the 1770s to the 1830s, there were large numbers of Scottish immigrants to the area. They were promised 200 acres of land when they arrived. At that time, this new land was considered to be part of Scotland.

Many of the former French settlers in Nova Scotia moved to Quebec, others went to Louisiana, and the British forcibly removed most of the rest.

The New Scottish and Scots-Irish settlers were located around the Bay of Fundy, Cape Breton Island, and along the coast of the Northumberland shores. They also settled on nearby Prince Edward Island. The Scottish Gaels tended to stick together, making their communities very homogenous. As a result, there was a very significant Scottish influence throughout Nova Scotia.

The new settlers were given two years to establish and maintain their land, with the aim of eventually becoming self-supporting.

The new immigrants spoke only the Gaelic language, and together they became the largest Gaelic cultural influence outside of Scotland. In 1900, the British decided to discourage the Gaelic language and forced the people to only speak English. If anyone was caught using Gaelic, whether written or spoken, they were punished.

Today, however, the Gaelic language around the islands, has been proudly resurrected, especially on Prince Edward Island, where, in areas, it is the primary language. A Gaelic school has been established on Cape Breton Island.

The English deliberately chose the Scots to settle in places like Nova Scotia, knowing that they were hardy, used to a simple lifestyle, and desired opportunity for economic improvement. Many were forced out of their homeland, some were tricked into moving, and others left eagerly, seeking a better life for their families.

Between 1770 and 1815, around 5,800 Scottish migrants had arrived in Nova Scotia. Their early homes were of the familiar croft style. It was a basic lifestyle similar to what they had in Scotland.

If they owned an animal such as a cow, it was usually kept inside during the winter months. After 1815, Scottish immigration came from the Lowland areas, and by 1870, 170,000 had arrived. The 1871 Canadian census showed that for every 1,000 Canadians, over 150 were of Scottish origin.

The climate was similar to what they had known, so most grew a variety of traditional crops with a high success rate. Fishing soon emerged to become a major industry. Halifax was established as a fishing port and naval station. Between 1850 and 1880, boat and shipbuilding also grew as an important and significant industry. From 1850 onward, coal mining in Nova Scotia became a major industry, as large coal seams had been discovered.

The Gaels who settled in Nova Scotia maintained strong kinship and religious ties. Many of the Scottish communities remain close-knit to the present. Today, Prince Edward Island is regarded as Canada's most Scottish Province.

Australia

Captain James Cook, the son of a Scottish ploughman, was the first Scottish link to Australia when he explored the continent in 1770. On his travels, he named two Pacific islands in honour of Scotland, These were the New Hebrides and New Caledonia. One of Cook's crew, a Scot from the Orkney Islands, was the first free Scot to die on Australian soil. He was buried at Botany Bay in New South Wales.

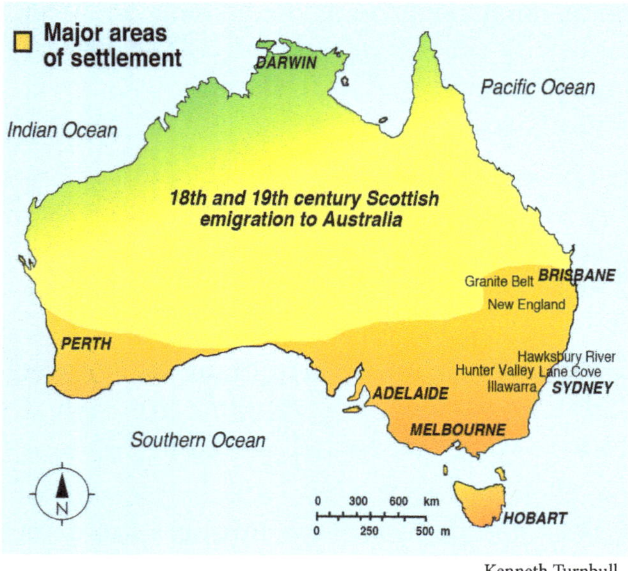

Kenneth Turnbull

Scottish settlement in Australia from 1778

The first Scottish settlers arrived in Australia on the 'First Fleet' in 1778, to establish a penal colony at Botany Bay. Most of the early Scottish settlers were convicts who had been deported and sent to Australia, for minor offences. Of the 150,000 convicts transported to Australia only 5% were Scottish. Most were English.

One such Scottish convict, a Turnbull, on the first fleet in 1803 to Van Diemen's Land (now Tasmania), had been transported for being drunk and disorderly.

The first Scottish free settlers were wealthy Lowlanders and some of the first merchants to migrate to the colonies. Others were skilled tradesmen and professionals, and they soon established themselves into the colony.

Twenty years later in 1798, the British Government offered incentives for those who chose to migrate as free settlers to Australia. There had been very few free settlers who emigrated to Australia in those first years, so the offer of free passage plus their food on the voyage of about six months, enticed many farmers and skilled workers.

Among those who accepted the offer, was John Turnbull, his wife Ann, and their family from Roxburghshire in the Borders. It soon became apparent that John with his wife and family of four would not be alone. Several of their friends also accepted the offer.

The Turnbulls, along with eight other families submitted their applications that included a list of their skills, personal references, and credentials. Their applications were accepted, and in February of 1802, they set sail in a ship of 522 tons, the *Coromandel,* for a new life in Australia. Convicts who were being transported to Australia also accompanied them on the ship. With a total number of 226, the journey was expected to take 175 days, yet good sailing conditions enabled the *Coromandel* to reach Port Jackson in a record 121 days non-stop from England.

A highly regarded Scottish minister, Reverend Alexander Waugh, who was either related to or a close friend with several of the Scottish families, accompanied them on the *Coromandel.*

On arrival, they were to be granted 100 acres of land near Port Jackson or 50 acres on Norfolk Island. They were also to be supplied with food, grain, agricultural tools, and clothing for twelve months. In addition, they would be assigned two prisoners as labourers, to help in establishing their farms. The government over the same period would provide the prisoners' keep.

In a few days, they packed and set off to Toongabbie, about 20 miles northwest of Port Jackson. There they were allocated land, where they began to clear and build a permanent shelter in which to live.

However, as that land proved to be very poor, rocky and unproductive, after only a few months, alternate land was provided further north from Sydney along the Hawkesbury River. This new land that the settlers chose proved more productive, and by April of the following year, John Turnbull had become the proud owner of 113 acres at Swallow Rock Reach. After several years, and by the time he died in 1834, he had extended his landholding to 200 acres.

After five years of house church worship, eight families contributed

£200 and covenanted to build a church and school. Ebenezer Church, which is still in use today, was completed in 1809. The well-chosen name means, 'The Lord has helped us all the way.' It is the simple barn style building preferred by the Nonconformist Scottish worshipers. In 2009, the bi-centenary of the Ebenezer Church, now Presbyterian, was celebrated.

Though land and farming were the original reasons for the Turnbulls and the others immigrating to the Hawkesbury in Australia, by the mid-19th century, their descendants were integrated into many areas of the emerging society.

Ebenezer Church, Ebenezer NSW, Australia

By the 1830s, more Scottish migrants had arrived in Australia due to the economic recession in Britain. Most were farmers, but all were educated and respected by the earlier free settlers. Because these new settlers were mostly from the areas of Edinburgh, Aberdeen and Dundee, they encouraged strong commercial ties between Scotland and Western Australia. They also settled in other growing cities, including Melbourne, Adelaide and Hobart.

Twenty years later when the Australian gold rush began, yet another 90,000 Scottish immigrants arrived in Australia. By 1860, they made up half of the population of the settlements around Australia.

New Zealand

As with Australia, Captain James Cook was the first Scottish link when he reached New Zealand in October 1769. Cook was the first European explorer to circumnavigate and map the islands of New Zealand. Captain Cook named the eastern tip of what is now known as Dunedin peninsula, Cape Saunders.

After Cook's exploration, New Zealand became regularly visited by adventurers, explorers, missionaries, and traders. In 1840, the Treaty of Waitangi was signed between the British Crown and the Māori, making New Zealand a part of the British Empire and giving Māori the same rights as other British subjects. Extensive English and Scottish settlements followed throughout the rest of the 19th and early 20th centuries.

The coastal town of Dunedin was founded by the Free Church of Scotland. The name (from *Dùn Èideann*, the Gaelic name for Edinburgh,) was given to the city because, on a map, it resembles the area around Edinburgh. The church leaders played a significant role in the city's development, principally as a Scottish settlement with housing characteristics designed to resemble those of their homeland. The architect, Thomas Turnbull, who immigrated to New Zealand from Glasgow, became well-known for his work in the colony.

Many lowland Scots immigrated to New Zealand as a result of the Agricultural Revolution. Having been part-time labourers and subtenants (cottars) they were forced to abandon their traditional system of farming to make way for new industrial practices. This ultimately resulted in high unemployment. A recent survey found that 60% of New Zealand's Scottish immigrants were from the lowlands, choosing to live in a climate similar to their new homeland.

The majority of Scottish immigrants settled in and around the South Island. They married Maori more readily than did the English and became known as 'Scottish New Zealanders,' sometimes called 'Pākehā.'

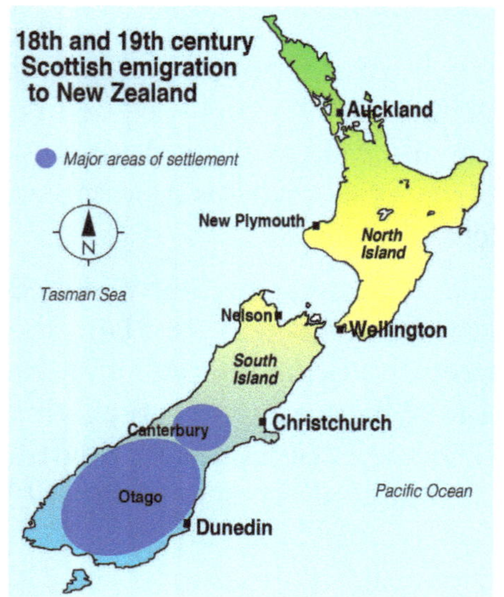

Jonny Robertson - CC 3.0

Clutha River and Roxburgh Bridge in Roxburgh, NZ named for long-gone but not forgotten Roxburgh, Scotland

Initially, there were five New Zealand Company Settlements; Wellington, Nelson, Auckland, Christchurch, and New Plymouth. From 1848, there was a second offer of assisted passage to immigrants, to Otago and Canterbury, although many of those settlers travelled across the Tasman Sea from Australia. This second flow of migrants contributed enormously to Auckland's population, with land grants of 40 acres being offered.

Caledonian societies were formed, which helped to keep the Scottish traditions and culture alive. However the Gaelic language of the Scots was not very popular, and as a result, it soon disappeared after just one generation.

The National Library of New Zealand was established through the bequest of Alexander Horsburgh Turnbull (1868-1918) with his extensive collection of literary and visual works. Amongst the collections, are the writings of English born poet, John Milton and his original poetic works of the 17th century, regarded as the finest collection in the world.

Four Men Who Shaped Scotland

William Wallace *Guardian of Scotland*–1272-1305

1272 - William Wallace is born in Elderslie, Scotland.

1290 - Faces hostilities from English soldiers, slays attackers.

1292 - Classed as a traitor and outlaw.

1297 - Strong in stature has grown to 6 feet 5 in height.

- Marries Marion a lady from Lanark who shortly after is murdered by local Sheriff as reprisal for William's exploits. William slays him.
- William appointed Guardian of Scotland.
- Leads and wins the Battle of Stirling Bridge.

1298 - William leads and loses the Battle of Falkirk.

- Resigns Guardian of Scotland.
- Flees to France as a fugitive.

1304 - William returns to Scotland and continues the struggle against the English.

1305 - Betrayed, apprehended and found guilty of high treason by England.

- Executed.

Robert the Bruce *King of Scots*–1274-1329

1274 - Robert the Bruce is born into a family of royalty.

1294 - Travels to Ireland.

1295 - Marries Isabella of Mar who dies in 1297.

1298 - Becomes Guardian of Scotland. Resigns two years later.

1302 - Marries Elizabeth de Burgh.

1306 - Crowned King of Scotland.

- Defeated by English occupation of Scotland. Goes into hiding in the Hebrides and Ireland.

1307 - Returns to Scotland. Defeats English at Louden Hill.

1308 - Gains control of most of northern Scotland.

1309 - Holds his first Scottish Parliament.

1310 - Has 14 military victories.

1313 - William 'o Rule turns wild charging bull, saves King Robert's life.

1314 - King Robert leads and wins the Battle of Bannockburn, the turning point in the First War of Scottish Independence.

1318 - Captures Berwick Upon Tweed.

1320 - Declaration of Arbroath.

1324 - Robert formally recognised as King of Scotland by the pope.

1326 - Franco-Scottish Alliance is formally created.

1328 - The Treaty of Edinburgh-Northampton is established.

1329 - King Robert the Bruce dies knowing that Scotland is an independent nation.

James Douglas *Sir James the Good*–1286-1330

1286 - James Douglas is born in Lanarkshire, the eldest son of William Douglas.

1296 - James witnesses the start of the First War of Scottish Independence.

- Threatens English soldiers with his knife, given by his father to protect his stepmother.

- Sent to France for safety.

- James is educated in Paris.

1298 - James father returns from English prison to family castle.

1304 - Douglas castle and land seized by English.

- James's petition for return of ancestral lands is rejected. He is angry and vows revenge.

- Becomes Commander in the First War of Scottish Independence.

1306 - Joins an alliance with King Robert the Bruce.

- Recognised as a brilliant tactician.

1307 - Attacks British troops and demolishes Douglas castle.

- Becomes known by the English as 'Black Douglas.'

1314 - James is knighted and fights as banneret at Bannockburn.

1330 - Sir James Douglas dies at the Battle of Teba in Andalucia, Spain.

William-'o-Rule *The First Turnbull*–1290-1333

1290 - William is born, in the Toon-'o'Roule, Roxburgh, Scotland.

1310 - William, strong in stature, has grown to over 6 ft in height.

1313 - William accompanies King Robert the Bruce on a royal hunting party to the Callendar Forest.

- William wrestles wounded wild bull charging the king and saves the king's life.

- William is given surname 'Turn-e-bull.'

- Granted the lands of Philiphaugh.

1314 - William takes part in the Battle of Bannockburn.

1333 - William challenges the English knight, Robert Benhale at the Battle of Halidon Hill and is killed along with his hound.

www.ingramcontent.com/pod-product-compliance
Lightning Source LLC
Chambersburg PA
CBHW051209090426
42740CB00021B/3430

9781611532067